JESUS & THE WAY OF SORROWS

NOBODY
LEFT
OUT

D1739092

A MESSY, BROKEN JOURNEY THROUGH
THE STATIONS OF THE CROSS

Edited by Emily Lupfer

Scriptures are italicized and are taken from the following versions of the Bible:

THE HOLY BIBLE, NEW INTERNATIONAL VERSION®, NIV® Copyright © 1973, 1978, 1984, 2011 by Biblica, Inc.® Used by permission. All rights reserved worldwide.

The Holy Bible, New Living Translation (NLT), copyright © 1996, 2004, 2015 by Tyndale House Foundation. Used by permission of Tyndale House Publishers, Inc., Carol Stream, Illinois 60188. All rights reserved.

Common English Bible®, CEB® Copyright © 2010, 2011 by Common English Bible.™ Used by permission. All rights reserved worldwide.

The Holy Bible, English Standard Version (ESV) is adapted from the Revised Standard Version of the Bible, copyright Division of Christian Education of the National Council of the Churches of Christ in the U.S.A. All rights reserved.

THE MESSAGE (MSG), copyright © 1993, 2002, 2018 by Eugene H. Peterson. Used by permission of NavPress. All rights reserved. Represented by Tyndale House Publishers, Inc.

Publishing services provided by  **Archangel Ink**

ISBN: 979-8-7131-3164-7

To anyone who has ever traveled down the Way of Sorrows.

May we be reminded that Jesus walks the broken road with us.

Nobody Left Out: Jesus Meets the Messes

Download 5 free sample chapters!

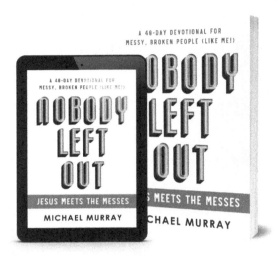

When Jesus walked this earth, he spent time with the messes.

This 40-day devotional looks at eight encounters Jesus had with messy, broken people. In short, daily readings, you'll explore each story and see how Jesus met each person in their mess.

Subscribe to the *Nobody Left Out* newsletter and you'll receive the first five chapters of the book for free!

Get it here:

NobodyLeftOut.net/Free

Contents

Introduction:
Traveling Down the Way of Sorrows

I love the victory of Easter Sunday.

I love gathering at church to celebrate the empty tomb. I love singing hope-filled songs about life winning out over death. As songwriter John Mark McMillan put it in one of my favorite songs, "The man Jesus Christ laid death in his grave."[1]

Because the occasion is so joyous, it's easy for me to brush aside the painful road Jesus journeyed to get there. I quickly forget that the beauty of Easter morning was preceded by horror. The road to the happy ending was paved with suffering. Easter proves that there is no victory without first death. There is no light without first darkness.

The Stations of the Cross Can Guide Us Along the Path of Suffering

The Stations of the Cross is a series of scenes that walk us through the events of Jesus' crucifixion and burial. They guide us down the path of the *Via Dolorosa*, the route in Jerusalem that Jesus walked on the day of his death. *Via Dolorosa* is Latin for "sorrowful way." Because of this, the Stations of the Cross is sometimes referred to as the Way of Sorrows. I like this term because it contrasts with the victory of Easter.

There are fourteen "stops" along the Way of Sorrows, beginning with Jesus sweating blood in a garden and ending with his burial. In between, there is a lot of pain, suffering, and despair.

---

1   John Mark McMillan. *Death in His Grave. The Medicine.* 2008.

While associated with Catholicism, the Stations of the Cross is a tradition observed in many Christian denominations. It's important to remember that we are not trying to earn God's love by going through the stations. Like any other devotional exercise, we should approach it as a tool to help us engage with God.

Tradition says that Mary was the first person to walk the Way of Sorrows. She would travel along the *Via Dolorosa*, remembering the sacrifice made by her son. While we don't know if this is true, I wouldn't be surprised if it is. We know that Mary was a woman who felt things deeply and pondered them in her heart. (Luke 2:19)

The Traditional Stations of the Cross

There are two "versions" of the Stations of the Cross: traditional and scriptural. Below are the fourteen stations of the Traditional Way. You might find images of this version in Catholic churches today.

1. Jesus is condemned to death
2. Jesus carries his cross
3. Jesus falls for the first time
4. Jesus meets his mother
5. Simon of Cyrene helps Jesus carry the cross
6. Veronica wipes the face of Jesus
7. Jesus falls for the second time
8. Jesus meets the women of Jerusalem
9. Jesus falls for the third time
10. Jesus is stripped of his clothes
11. Jesus is nailed to the cross
12. Jesus dies on the cross
13. Jesus is taken down from the cross
14. Jesus is placed in the tomb

Of the fourteen scenes above, only eight are depicted in the Bible. The other six are based on church tradition. These six scenes are:

Stations 3, 7, and 9: The Three Times Jesus Falls

Although not recorded in Scripture, I wouldn't be surprised if Jesus collapsed in exhaustion during his journey.

Station 4: Jesus Meets His Mother Along the Road

In this scene, Mary and Jesus meet and lock eyes for a brief moment. Although not recorded in any gospel account, it's a moving scene that captures the anguish of a mother about to watch her son die.

Station 6: Veronica Wipes the Face of Jesus

This is a wild story! According to legend, Veronica—an ordinary woman from Jerusalem—gave her veil to Jesus so he could wipe his sweat-covered face. After handing the veil back to her, Veronica saw an impression of Jesus' face on it![2] This story has no biblical basis and did not pop up in writings until the Middle Ages. *Hmmm...* I wonder if this is where the legends began of seeing Jesus' face in weird places, like on your toast!

Station 13: Jesus Is Taken Down From the Cross

Although Jesus was taken down from the cross, the details found in Scripture differ from this account. In the Bible, Joseph of Arimathea takes down Jesus' body to prepare it for burial. But in this traditional version, Jesus' lifeless body is laid in Mary's arms, which is not found anywhere in Scripture.

---

2 "Saint Veronica." *Wikipedia*, Wikimedia Foundation, en.wikipedia.org/wiki/Saint_Ve ronica.

The Scriptural Stations of the Cross

On Good Friday in 1991, Pope John Paul II unveiled the Scriptural Stations of the Cross. In this new version, each scene is based on an account written in the Gospels.[3]

I prefer this version over the traditional because it allows us to read each scene as we contemplate it. We can travel along the Way of Sorrows with Jesus and see it all play out in our imaginations. We huddle quietly in the courtroom as Pilate tries Jesus. We feel the shame when Peter denies Jesus. We embrace the hope when Jesus welcomes the thief on the cross.

Below are the fourteen stations of the Scriptural Way. I have included the corresponding passage of Scripture for each one.

1. Jesus in the Garden of Gethsemane (Mark 14:32-42)
2. Jesus is betrayed by Judas and arrested (John 18:1-13; Luke 22:47-53)
3. Jesus is condemned by the Sanhedrin (Mark 14:53–65)
4. Jesus is denied by Peter (Matthew 26:69-75)
5. Jesus is judged by Pilate (John 18:28-19:16)
6. Jesus is scourged and crowned with thorns (Mark 15:15-20)
7. Jesus takes up his cross (John 19:16-17)
8. Jesus is helped by Simon of Cyrene to carry his cross (Matthew 27:32, Mark 15:21, Luke 23:26)
9. Jesus meets the women of Jerusalem (Luke 23:27-31)
10. Jesus is crucified (Mark 15:23-32)
11. Jesus promises his kingdom to the repentant thief (Luke 23:39-43)
12. Jesus entrusts Mary and John to each other (John 19:25-27)
13. Jesus dies on the cross (Mark 15:33-39)
14. Jesus is placed in the tomb (Matthew 27:57-61)

---

3   Wilson, Ralph F. "Scriptural Way of the Cross or Biblical Stations of the Cross Introduced by Pope John Paul II." *Joyful Heart Renewal Ministries*, www.joyfulheart.com /stations-of-the-cross/scriptural-way-of-the-cross.htm.

What About the Resurrection?

In both versions, the fourteenth and final station is Jesus' body resting in the tomb. Some have argued that without the resurrection, the story of Jesus is incomplete. Because of this, a fifteenth station is sometimes added depicting the empty tomb.

People who argue against a fifteenth station say that the Way of Sorrows is not meant to tell the entire story. The purpose is to highlight Jesus' suffering as he traveled down the *Via Dolorosa*.

I see merits in both views. Celebrating the victory of Jesus' resurrection seems like an appropriate way to conclude his journey! To that end, I have included a chapter on the fifteenth station in this book.

Journeying With Jesus

In the following pages, we're going to travel down the Way of Sorrows with Jesus. (We'll use the Scriptural version.) It won't be a pretty sight. We will see our Savior broken. We will see the man who fed 5000, healed the sick, and walked on water in a helpless state. We will see a friend who loved deeply get spit on and mocked.

But before we begin the journey, I want to give three reasons why I think it's helpful to walk down this road of suffering with Jesus.

1. It Reminds Us That Jesus Understands Suffering

Each one of us is traveling down our own *Via Dolorosa*. It could be dealing with a health issue, a family crisis, or a feeling of isolation and abandonment. At some point, we all look up to the heavens and cry out, "Why, God?! Why is this happening to me?!"

Theologically, there *are* answers to that question. But let's be honest— no explanation will ever be good enough for me. I may be able to understand my suffering on some intellectual level, but I still won't be okay with it. The pain will always be there.

5

The Way of Sorrows is an explicit reminder that God entered into our suffering. I may not understand pain, but I know Jesus is in it with me. He chose to enter the mess and put himself into the hands of selfish, agenda-pushing humans. That's not something I would want to do!

When I walk down the Way of Sorrows with Jesus, I begin to realize that Jesus is walking down the Way of Sorrows with me.

2. It Reminds Us of How Much We Are Loved

Why did Jesus walk down this Way of Sorrows when he could have avoided it? Because he loves us. And not just the collective "us," but the individual "us." Jesus loves *you*.

As we journey along the *Via Dolorosa*, there'll be times we want to look away. It's all too much to take in. But Jesus endured every scar, every insult, and every nail for you and me. And not with the purpose of making us feel guilty enough to "behave." It's a much bigger vision than that! He endured it so we can break free of anything keeping us from living the life we were made to live. We can love others, knowing we are loved.

3. It Reminds Us That Suffering Has an Expiration Date

Suffering may be a universal experience, but it's not going to last forever. The Way of Sorrows has an end. That fifteenth station is coming! The empty tomb is good news for us all. It's proof that God doesn't want anyone left out. Jesus put death in its grave, and one day he'll put our suffering there too.

Walking down the Way of Sorrows with Jesus is not a comfortable journey. But it's a journey where light glimmers in darkness, and hope peeks out from despair.

We know the story ends with a victorious sunrise on Easter morning.

Travel Tips
(How to Use This Book)

This book is not an exhaustive study of the Stations of the Cross, but a brief overview. Each chapter is devoted to one station, or "scene," from Jesus' journey to the cross.

I tried to focus on one main idea for each station. My hope is that these short chapters will be a starting point for exploring the drama of the cross. So much more could be said about each vignette. That's why I love the Bible. You can read the same story again and again and learn something new each time. As you read these stories, I encourage you to bring your own unique perspective to them!

Before we begin our journey down the Way of Sorrows, here are a few travel tips to help you get ready...

* There is no "right time" to use this book. Many people use the Stations of the Cross to guide them through the Lenten season (the 46 days leading up to Easter). This book could be used as a devotional tool during Lent, but you could also use it any other time of the year. So feel free to take the journey whenever you would like!

* As I mentioned, each chapter covers one station. Although the chapters are short, I'd recommend only reading one chapter per day. (Or one every few days.) Jesus' journey to the cross is a heavy topic. If we try to rush through it, we might miss the chance to embrace the fullness of the story. Take your time. Feel free to sit in each station for as long as you need to. Yes, the journey can

get dark. The Way of Sorrows is a messy, broken road. But that's good news. It means Jesus traveled it for messy, broken people!

* At the beginning of each chapter, I'll give the Scripture reference for where you can find that station's story in the Bible. I suggest taking a few minutes to read the full passage before diving into the chapter.

* If you're looking for a quick, easy way to access the Bible, consider downloading the YouVersion Bible App. Another great resource is BibleGateway.com.

* At the end of each chapter, I've included some questions to ponder. As with everything in this book, use them in whatever way is most helpful to you. My hope is they will give you something to reflect on as you sit in each station. You may connect with some more deeply than others.

* Last but not least (probably most important!): No matter how you decide to engage with the Stations of the Cross, remember it's a tool to guide you, not an obligation to burden you. We don't earn "God Points" by reading the Bible. As we'll soon see from the journey he walked for us, there's nothing we can do to make Jesus love us any more than he already does. Our goal is just to get to know him better!

Okay, all packed and ready to go?

Our journey along the *Via Dolorosa* begins on a dark night in a quiet garden...

Station I:
The Garden of Suffering

Station I of the Stations of the Cross: Jesus in the Garden of Gethsemane.
Bible Reading: Mark 14:32-42

There is a scene in the movie *Superman* that has stuck with me since I was a kid.

The evil genius Lex Luthor has launched nuclear missiles toward two U.S. cities. Superman finds Luthor's hideout and demands Luthor hand over the detonator. As he searches for it, Luthor tricks Superman into opening a box of kryptonite.

We see the fear in Superman's eyes as he gazes at the glowing piece of green rock. The Man of Steel, once so confident, melts into a puddle of weakness at the hands of the evil villain. With Superman's powers restrained, Luthor is able to effortlessly push him into a pool.

The scene is memorable because of how vulnerable our hero becomes. It's not fun to see Superman flailing helplessly in a pool when he should be saving humanity. When Superman is standing tall, I'm not worried if aliens from Krypton are trying to take over the world. He's got things covered. But if Superman looks afraid, then I'm terrified!

I get a similar feeling of uneasiness when I read about Jesus in the Garden of Gethsemane. The Garden is the first stop along the Way of Sorrows. It is the quiet before the storm and the place where we see Jesus at his most human. Maybe a little *too human* for our tastes.

Jesus Embraces Sadness & Fear

Jesus and his disciples go to Gethsemane after eating the Last Supper. (Gethsemane means "oil press" in Aramaic.[4] It was a garden filled with olive trees.) When they arrive, Jesus takes his three closest disciples—Peter, James, and John—aside. Jesus is feeling anxious and desires the companionship of his friends. He confides in them, "I'm very sad. It's as if I'm dying. Stay here and keep alert" (Mark 14:34, CEB).

Jesus was very sad.

There is a stigma around sadness, especially among Christians. We think we shouldn't be sad because we have "victory in Christ." But here we see Jesus give in to the weight of grief. If we deny our sadness, then we're denying part of our humanity—a part Jesus embraced.

Then Jesus leaves his friends to go pray by himself. What kind of prayer do we expect Jesus to pray?

Thank you, Father, for this awesome challenge.

Or, *Yes, I know I can handle whatever's coming with you by my side.*

But that's not the prayer Jesus prays. Instead, he utters words we might say:

Abba, Father, everything is possible for you. Please take this cup of suffering away from me. (v. 36, NLT)

Jesus is terrified about what's to come. He knows the agony he's about to endure, and he's not looking at it through "holy-colored" lenses. His prayer isn't, "God, get me through this." It's, "God, get me out of this!"

---

4 "GETHSEMANE." Experience the Land of the Bible, www.land-of-the-bible.com/Geth semane.

We All Know Suffering

We have all wanted God to get us out of something. It could be a ninth grader praying for her teacher to cancel the math quiz. Or a cancer patient praying for different lab results.

My suffering isn't the same as your suffering, and it doesn't do much good to debate whose pain is worse. But we can empathize with each other. We can be sad with each other.

In Luke's telling of this story, he adds this detail:

And being in anguish, [Jesus] prayed more earnestly, and his sweat was like drops of blood falling to the ground. (Luke 22:44, NIV)

Luke was a doctor, and he wanted us to know the physical manifestation of Jesus' anxiety. Beads of sweat as thick as blood droplets ran down Jesus' face.

In Gethsemane, Jesus shows us he doesn't like suffering any more than we do. On his knees, Jesus doesn't look like Superman. He looks like me. He looks like you.

"Please take this cup of suffering away from me."

It's okay for us to pray this prayer. I've prayed it several times throughout my life.

But Jesus doesn't end the prayer there. He tacks on another sentence. It's a sentence I leave out of my prayers because I don't have the courage to pray it.

[Jesus added,] "Yet I want your will to be done, not mine." (v. 36, NLT)

Jesus was willing to face the suffering head-on if that's what God wanted of him. When he hears the rustling of soldiers approaching, he decides to face whatever comes next. Instead of hiding, he steps out into the open and tells his friends to brace themselves.

"The time has come for the Human One to be betrayed into the hands of sinners. Get up! Let's go! Look, here comes my betrayer." (v. 41-42, CEB)

What's the Lesson of Gethsemane?

I used to think the lesson of Gethsemane was to be like Jesus and face our suffering bravely. We should "drink the cup," even when we don't want to. But I'm not sure that's the case.

Between prayers in Gethsemane, Jesus went back to the spot where he left his friends. Maybe he wanted their encouragement. But every time he did, he would find them asleep.

*Then he returned and found the disciples asleep. He said to Peter, "Simon, are you asleep? Couldn't you watch with me even one hour? Keep watch and pray, so that you will not give in to temptation. **For the spirit is willing, but the body is weak.**"* (v. 37-38, NLT, emphasis mine)

When Jesus says the body is weak, I don't think he's being critical. He's being truthful.

Jesus knows my spirit may be committed to following him, but my body is weak.

We are tired. We are weary.

I want to wake up at 5 a.m. each morning and devote two hours to prayer and Bible reading. But my body is weak.

I want to volunteer more and help my community. My body is weak.

I want to face trials and suffering with maturity and patience. But my body is oh, so weak.

I want to drink the bitter cup of suffering as Jesus did, but I can't bring myself to do it. I'm far too weak.

Gethsemane reminds us that Jesus drank the cup for us. He knew Peter and the rest of his friends would soon abandon him. And yet he faced the agony of the cross for them. And us.

Does This Mean We Don't Have to Face Suffering?

I wish!

It means Jesus is in our suffering *with us*. It means Jesus is our strength when we're weak. It means it's okay to feel sad, afraid, and lonely because Jesus felt those things too.

It means when we are in our own Gethsemane, praying for the cup to pass us by, we are not alone. Jesus is there, keeping watch. He kneels beside us, wraps one arm around us, and with the other takes the cup from our hands.

And, with beads of sweat dripping down his forehead, he looks at us and says, "I will drink this with you."

🗨 Questions to Ponder:

Is Jesus' fear and anguish in the garden surprising to you in any way? How can you relate to it?

What "cup of suffering" do you wish God would take away from you? How can you remind yourself that Jesus is in the suffering with you, even if God doesn't take it away?

What is one thing you learned about Jesus from this station?

13

Station II:
Sword Wielders & Ear Healers

Station II of the Stations of the Cross: Jesus is betrayed by Judas and arrested.
Bible Reading: John 18:1-13, Luke 22:47-53

When the other disciples saw what was about to happen, they exclaimed, "Lord, should we fight? We brought the swords!" And one of them struck at the high priest's slave, slashing off his right ear. But Jesus said, "No more of this." And he touched the man's ear and healed him. (Luke 22:49-51, NLT)

When the high priest's servant woke up on the morning of Jesus' arrest, I doubt he thought his ear would be chopped off by an overzealous fisherman. But later that night, he found his life changed forever.

In John's gospel, we learn this servant's name is Malchus. All four gospels include this story, but only John names the servant. John knew the high priest (John 18:15), so it makes sense that he would know the names of the people associated with him. (Little details like this are what I find so fascinating about the Bible!)

Jesus' arrest is our second stop along the Way of Sorrows. After the quiet moments of prayer in Gethsemane, the scene breaks into chaos. Judas, a close friend of Jesus, guides a group of soldiers and officials to the garden to make the arrest.

When I picture this scene play out, I imagine a small group of soldiers coming to arrest Jesus. He's one man who travels with a group of 12 nobodies—how much muscle do they really need? But the Greek language suggests a group of 600-1,000 men—and they were armed and ready to fight.

The group was mostly made up of chief priests and Jewish temple guards. But the high priest also managed to convince a few Roman soldiers to go along on the midnight raid. It was Passover and Rome was on high alert, ready to quash any chaos that may bubble up.

There are many things to highlight in this story. The way Judas betrays Jesus with a kiss. The group of 600 soldiers cowering in fear when Jesus speaks. Jesus' compassion and concern for his friends. But today, I want to focus on Malchus.

As the servant of the high priest, it was Malchus's job to make sure Jesus was arrested. The operation fell on him, and if anything went wrong, he'd be held responsible.

As soldiers are shouting and chaos is swirling, Peter does something drastic. He grabs a sword and lobs off Malchus's right ear.

Was Peter's Act Courageous?

Some commentators say even though Peter was wrong to start swinging swords, he was at least showing courage. Surrounded by 600 soldiers, he was ready to fight to the death for Jesus.

Other commentators say it was more of a cheap shot. Because it was the right ear that got mangled, some surmise Peter attacked Malchus from behind. And because Malchus wasn't a soldier, he was probably unarmed.

I guess my question is, *what is courage?* Is it simply doing something that scares you, no matter what it is? Or is it something more?

Right before he attacks Malchus, Peter asks Jesus, "Lord, should we fight?" But he doesn't wait for an answer.

15

Would it have been more courageous of Peter to show restraint? We get the sense Peter was swinging the sword around like a maniac, the way a child would roughhouse with a toy sword. He was aiming for Malchus's head and instead got a piece of an ear.

This Is Where the Garden of Gethsemane Intersects With Our Own Lives

Peter saw Malchus as the enemy who was out to stop Jesus.

Who do we see as the enemy? Who are we swinging swords at like a maniac?

No, we may not be wielding real swords, but we wield verbal ones. We wield digital ones. And we do it all in the name of defending what's right.

It's become a bit of a cliché to say we are divided. But I don't think that's our main problem. There will always be differences of opinion. The problem is when we view those who disagree with us as "the enemy."

Yesterday, I came across a cartoon of a man sitting in a psychiatrist's office. The caption reads: "Life was beautiful. Then I read the comments."

Have you ever seen a Facebook comment thread turn toxic? The conversation stops being about the topic at hand and turns into personal attacks and generalizations about specific groups of people. (I shouldn't just pick on Facebook. This happens on blog posts, articles, and other social media platforms, too.)

I get stressed whenever I see a heated comment thread, and yet I feel compelled to jump in and start swinging my own sword.

Isn't it amazing how much your blood can boil just by reading other people's opinions? And that's the worst time to pick up a sword because you have no control over yourself.

I end up chopping off empathy and understanding. I end up chopping off love, kindness, and the chance at a genuine relationship.

I continue the cycle of manic sword swinging.

No More of This

In the middle of the chaos, Jesus steps in. Jesus is always willing to step into our mess and show us a better way.

"No more of this," he says. Then he heals Malchus's ear and allows himself to be arrested.

For one brief moment, Malchus's life was changed as his ear got lobbed off. Fear washed over him as he thought about what that would mean for the rest of his life.

Then, just as quickly, his life was changed again when Jesus healed him. And even though Malchus still carried out his marching orders, I don't think he was ever the same. Dr. Ralph F. Wilson speculates on Malchus's future:

I wonder if Malchus is ever able to forget the sensation of Jesus' hand on the side of his bloody face. One minute he feels excruciating pain, the next, peace and wholeness. This emissary of the high priest must do his duty and take his healer into custody, but how can he ever be the same? Maybe the reason John mentions his name is because later he becomes a disciple and is known to the Christian community. We just don't know.[5]

---

5   Wilson, Ralph F. "Jesus' Arrest." *JesusWalk Bible Study Series*, www.jesuswalk.com /luke/100-arrest.htm.

Kindness and Compassion Always Go Further Than Hate and Viciousness

Sometimes I'll see a negative Facebook thread take a positive turn because of a kind response. Someone will have empathy toward a person they disagree with. They'll ask a sincere question, or change the mood with a lighthearted joke. And the connection becomes more human. It's as if they have reattached an ear!

There are a lot of people walking around right now with missing ears. They've been bloodied by the fight, and now they've picked up a sword in retaliation.

There are people walking around with wounds we know nothing about.

They seem angry, but the anger is covering their hurt. They've been hurt by others. Maybe by some who claim to follow Jesus. And now they are on guard.

How can we put down our swords and show them kindness?

I pray that Jesus will give me the courage to be an ear healer.

🗩 Questions to Ponder:

How would you define courage? Do you think Peter showed courage in Gethsemane?

When are you most prone to wield swords at people? What do you think it looks like to be an "ear healer"?

What is one thing you learned about Jesus from this station?

Station III:
When Hatred Takes Control

Station III of the Stations of the Cross: Jesus is condemned by the Sanhedrin.
Bible Reading: Mark 14:53-65

Then some of them began to spit at [Jesus], and they blindfolded him and beat him with their fists. "Prophesy to us," they jeered. And the guards slapped him as they took him away. (Mark 14:65, NLT)

Can you remember the last time you got really angry? I mean, so angry that you felt it well up from deep inside your stomach, and there was nothing you could do to stop it from unleashing?

What causes this kind of anger?

Sometimes we get angry when we see injustices happening around us. This type of anger can be useful if it propels us towards good deeds. Still, those good deeds will probably be more effective if we first gain control over our anger.

Most of the time, our anger comes from less noble pursuits. We want something, and we're not getting it. So we go bonkers when the waiter brings us an unsweet tea even though we asked for sweet. *(Totally made-up scenario...)*

Then there is a third type of anger. It is also rooted in selfishness, but it doesn't end there. This anger bursts forth when we sow seeds of hatred in our hearts.

This anger is dangerous because it charades itself as "righteous anger." If not dealt with, it can be used to justify horrible acts. I believe this is the kind of anger we see on display when Jesus is put on trial before the Sanhedrin.

This "trial" (if you can call it that) is our third stop along the Way of Sorrows. After Jesus' midnight arrest, he is taken to the Sanhedrin, a 71-member court. This court was comprised of "all the chief priests, elders, and legal experts" (v. 53, CEB).

The Sanhedrin had no real legal power from a "state" perspective. They ruled over religious matters. If things got *really* dicey, they could send people to the governor of Rome for a formal trial.

The Sanhedrin commonly held court in the temple. But when they arrested Jesus, they quietly gathered at the home of Caiaphas, the high priest. There, under cover of night, they were able to give full vent to their anger.

And boy, were they angry. Jesus had publicly criticized these religious leaders. He called them out on their hypocrisy and the way they twisted the law to puff themselves up.

In the weeks leading up to his arrest, the Pharisees tried to deal with Jesus in the daylight. They threw out trick questions to trap him, but each answer he gave amazed the crowd. He seemed unstoppable.

But now the tables were turned. They had Jesus hidden away in a place where they could do whatever they wanted to him. And their hatred was turned up to full volume.

The hatred these men harbored allowed them to justify three actions. If we're not careful, our hatred can lead us to these same justifications.

1. Hatred Justifies Deception

Why did the Sanhedrin meet in the middle of the night at Caiaphas's house rather than the public square? They were planning a deception. They were holding a fake trial with fake witnesses.

Some commentators suggest not all 71 members of the council were present that night. It was a secret meeting attended only by the leaders who wanted to stop Jesus at any cost.

Lou Nicholes describes how many rules the Sanhedrin had to break to achieve their goal:

The Sanhedrin was required to hold its hearings in the hall of stones in the temple, but Jesus was tried in the private residences of Annas and Caiaphas. A case could not be tried at night, yet Jesus was tried at night. A person was not to be tried on a feast day, yet Jesus was tried during Passover... The witnesses had to agree, but these witnesses did not agree. Jesus was convicted before He was tried.[6]

How were these men able to justify this shady behavior? Their hatred for Jesus convinced them it had to be done. It was for the greater good, they reasoned.

When hatred takes control, it opens the door to doing whatever needs to be done to push our agenda forward.

2. Hatred Justifies Violence

When hatred leads to deception, it's often on a slow boil. It takes time and patience to plot out a plan.

But hatred can also lead to an instant loss of composure.

Imagine being called into a meeting with leaders at your church to discuss something you did. Things get a little heated, so you turn

---

6   Nicholes, Lou. "Jesus Is Brought Before The Sanhedrin." *Family Times*, www.family-ti mes.net/commentary/mark-14-53/.

to leave the room. You feel one of them grab you from behind and throw you down to the ground. They each take turns punching you in the face.

Sounds horrific, right?

That's what the Sanhedrin did to Jesus after they pronounced him guilty. These learned, dignified men were so consumed with hate for Jesus that they brutally beat him.

We make jokes about going into "Hulk mode," but that's what these guys did. And it wasn't a pretty sight.

In 2014, Aliah Hernandez was brutally beaten by a man after telling him she was a transgender woman. Hernandez recalls the rage her attacker flew into:

"He said, 'I hate transsexuals, whatever you are,'" Hernandez recounted. "He hit me with his elbows, and he knocked me down on the floor. And then, he went crazy. He hit me on the floor really bad and tried to choke me and everything. And he just kept screaming, 'You're gonna die tonight. You're gonna die, you're gonna die.'"[7]

Notice the language used by the attacker. *"Whatever* you are."

When hatred takes control, we're able to dehumanize others. And when we dehumanize others, horrific acts of violence are not far behind.

3. Hatred Justifies Injustice

If you allow hatred to go on long enough, it stops looking like hate and starts looking like business as usual. This is not the kind of hatred

---

7   Daniari, Serena. "Transgender Woman Aliah Hernandez Was Brutally Beaten and Left for Dead. Her Attacker Walked Free." *Mic*, 21 Nov. 2018, www.mic.com/articles/1925 73/transgender-woman-aliah-hernandez-was-brutally-beaten-and-left-for-dead-her-att acker-walked-free.

that flies into an uncontrollable rage and does instant damage. It's a calculated hatred, quietly working its way into everyday systems.

The morning after Jesus' bloody trial, the Sanhedrin reconvenes. Having got their rage out the night before, they now move onto more practical matters.

Very early in the morning the leading priests, the elders, and the teachers of religious law—the entire high council—met to discuss their next step. They bound Jesus, led him away, and took him to Pilate, the Roman governor. (Mark 15:1, NLT)

The physical violence against Jesus was cathartic, but they still needed a way to get rid of him legally. So they call a meeting with all 71 members of the council and work out a way to bring formal charges against him.

If we really hate someone, the best way to oppress them is to work through legal avenues. Because then, we don't have to admit to hating anyone. We can hide behind systems. We can say, "Well, I wish it were different, but this is just the way things are."

When hatred takes control, we begin to create systems of injustice where hate masks itself as rational bureaucracy.

* * *

This story is kind of a downer, huh? It shows that our journey along the *Via Dolorosa* will not get any easier from here.

It's discouraging to see how hatred can poison the world, and even more discouraging to see how it poisons my own heart. It's hard to admit, but the effects of hatred are alive and well in my life. I'm not immune to it. I call private meetings of the Sanhedrin in the chambers of my heart all the time. We gather in the darkness and pass judgments on people.

Is there any hope?

If there's one thing the Way of Sorrows teaches us, it's that with Jesus, there's always hope in the darkness. But it starts by admitting we can't fix our anger issues on our own. We need to look to Jesus to find a better way.

Jesus' Silence Saved Us

Throughout this whole phony trial, Jesus remains silent. As the religious leaders grow furious, Jesus does not attempt to defend himself. The only time Jesus speaks is when the high priest asks him, "Are you the Messiah, the Son of the Blessed One?" (v. 61, NLT)

Whenever the Pharisees asked Jesus a question, his answer would turn the issue back on them. He would reveal a hole in their logic or point out their hypocrisy. But this time, Jesus was stunningly direct in his response:

Jesus said, "I am. And you will see the Son of Man seated in the place of power at God's right hand and coming on the clouds of heaven." (v. 62, NLT)

When Jesus says, "I am," he's describing himself the same way God did when he spoke to Moses in the burning bush centuries earlier. And this sent the high priest into a rage.

As the Sanhedrin heaped violence upon Jesus, he remained silent. And in that silence, he was paying the cost for their anger and hatred. Hundreds of years earlier, the prophet Isaiah predicted this would happen:

He was oppressed and afflicted,
*   yet he did not open his mouth;*
he was led like a lamb to the slaughter,
*   and as a sheep before its shearers is silent,*
*   so he did not open his mouth. (Isaiah 53:7, NIV)*

The next time I feel the twinge of anger rise in me, I hope I remember the price Jesus paid for it. Before I fan the flames further, I hope I will give it over to Jesus. He's the only one who can transform anger and hatred into peace and love.

💬 Questions to Ponder:

How have you seen hatred justify deception, violence, and injustice in culture? What about in your own life?

When are you most tempted to call private meetings of the Sanhedrin in the chambers of your heart? How can you hand those meetings over to Jesus instead?

What is one thing you learned about Jesus from this station?

Station IV:
Be Thankful When the Rooster Crows

Station IV of the Stations of the Cross: Jesus is denied by Peter. Bible Reading: Matthew 26:69-75

Have you ever started the day feeling confident, hopping out of bed, ready to conquer the world? Then by lunchtime, the stressors of the day have already overwhelmed you and you're ready to crawl back under the covers? You think back to who you were a few short hours ago and wonder, *What happened? Where did I go wrong?*

If you've ever felt that way, you're in good company. Jesus' friend Peter knows how you feel.

Peter's denial of Jesus is our fourth stop along the Way of Sorrows. It overlaps with Station III. While the Sanhedrin is questioning Jesus, Peter is out in the courtyard, denying he's ever met him.

Just a few hours earlier, at the Last Supper, Peter had pledged complete loyalty to Jesus.

Peter said, "Lord, I am ready to go to prison with you, and even to die with you." But Jesus said, "Peter, let me tell you something. Before the rooster crows tomorrow morning, you will deny three times that you even know me." (Luke 22:33-34, NLT)

I don't know about you, but if Jesus told me I would deny him three times, I'd be pretty disheartened. His words seem harsh, but maybe they are a blessing. Jesus knows Peter will fail, and yet he's still offering him a seat at the table. It's a reminder that Jesus knows all our flaws better than we do. He knows them, and he loves us. (I was tempted to tack on an "anyway" at the end of that sentence, but I don't think I need to. Jesus doesn't love us *despite* our warts, but *with them*.)

Jesus' warning seems to go right over Peter's head. He's confident he will stick with Jesus until the end. And, as we saw in Station II, Peter jumps into action at Jesus' arrest and cuts off the ear of the high priest's servant. In Peter's mind, he's making good on his oath of loyalty.

But then Peter sees the soldiers tie up Jesus and lead him away. The disciples' efforts to defend Jesus have failed. Now things are getting real. Maybe for Peter, things start feeling *surreal*. He follows the parade of soldiers to the home of the high priest. Unsure of what to do next, he hangs back in the courtyard as Jesus is taken inside.

Overtaken by Fear

When was the last time you were gripped by fear?

Fear does something to us. When fight-or-flight kicks in, we feel the rush of adrenaline and an increased heart rate. We'll do whatever it takes to get out of the situation, and I think for most of us, flight is the option we choose.

I would be a terrible character in a horror movie because I would never allow the plot to advance.

"Wanna spend the weekend at the abandoned cabin in the woods?" *Nope.*

"Wanna go to the cemetery on Halloween?" *I'll pass.*

"I think there's a shark in the ocean." *I'm outta here.*

Movie over before it begins.

This is the kind of fear that gripped Peter in the courtyard. He was so afraid that a comment from a servant girl sent him into a panic.

Meanwhile, Peter was sitting outside in the courtyard. A servant girl came over and said to him, "You were one of those with Jesus the Galilean." But Peter denied it in front of everyone. "I don't know what you're talking about," he said. (Matthew 26:69-70, NLT)

Why did the servant girl question Peter about knowing Jesus? Was she trying to get Peter in trouble? Or was it out of curiosity? There was so much excitement surrounding Jesus that night. Maybe she wanted to hear what went down from a firsthand source.

No matter what her motivation was, her words startled Peter. The man who drew his sword in the sight of hundreds of soldiers was now speechless when the topic of Jesus came up.

What was Peter scared of? Was he afraid he'd be arrested like Jesus and sentenced to death? Was he afraid of the blows the temple guards might inflict on him?

I don't blame Peter for being frightened out of his mind. I'd be too.

Jesus Knows How Scary the World Is

Throughout their time together, Jesus reminded his disciples not to be afraid. You only need that reminder if there are scary things out there.

Maybe Peter thought back to the day when a big storm broke out while Jesus and the disciples were on a boat. They were terrified to see Jesus napping while lightning flashed and thunder cracked. They woke him up in a panic.

Jesus responded, "Why are you afraid? You have so little faith!" Then he got up and rebuked the wind and waves, and suddenly there was a great calm. (Matthew 8:26, NLT)

Things always had a way of working out when Jesus was around.

But right now, Jesus seems so far away to Peter. As he mills about the high priest's courtyard, he feels alone. And he has the feeling he's in too deep. Maybe Peter was thinking, *If Jesus allowed himself to be arrested, then this really could be the end.*

Peter denies knowing Jesus two more times. Each denial becomes more desperate. By the last denial, Peter loses all composure and screams in frustration.

Peter swore, "A curse on me if I'm lying—I don't know the man!" And immediately the rooster crowed. (Matthew 26:74, NLT)

The crow of the rooster snaps Peter back into reality. Luke tells us after the rooster crows, Peter and Jesus lock eyes for a moment.

At that moment, the Lord turned and looked at Peter. Suddenly, the Lord's words flashed through Peter's mind: "Before the rooster crows tomorrow morning, you will deny three times that you even know me." And Peter left the courtyard, weeping bitterly. (Luke 22:61-62, NLT)

Healed by the Grace of Tears

I can't imagine how heartbreaking it was for Peter to see Jesus right after his third denial. At this point, it's morning, and the religious leaders are sending Jesus to Pilate for a formal trial. Jesus' face is bloodied from the beating he took the night before. As Peter sees his friend in this helpless state, he fills with shame. And he begins weeping uncontrollably.

Have you ever felt so broken that you wept bitterly like Peter?

I'm an ugly crier, I admit it. When I start wailing, I can't stop, and you won't be able to understand a word I'm saying. I'm the kind of crier who causes a scene at Starbucks.

The times I weep loudest are when I feel like a failure. I've let somebody down. I've messed up in some way. I've disappointed God. And it feels like there's no way I can redeem myself.

Tears can be ugly, but they can also be beautiful.

I believe tears are a grace from God. They remind us things are not yet as they should be. We cry when we feel broken, and that's because we *are* broken.

Peter wept because he fell short of who he wanted to be. He wanted to come through for Jesus in his time of need. He wanted to make Jesus proud, and that's understandable. If we love Jesus, we want to make him proud.

Peter wanted to be Jesus' savior. But through his tears, Peter realized *he* needed a savior. And Jesus had that covered.

As Peter was denying Jesus in the courtyard, Jesus was inside, confessing to the "crime" of being the Son of God. Where Peter showed weakness, Jesus showed strength.

Jesus wasn't surprised by Peter's denial. It didn't catch him off guard or throw a wrench into his plans. He predicted it, and he loved Peter enough to die for him.

In the same way, Jesus isn't surprised by our missteps or failures. He loves us.

Be Thankful When the Rooster Crows

Peter realized how broken he was when the rooster crowed. We all have moments when we are snapped back into reality and remember how much we fall short in life.

So what do we do when we hear the proverbial rooster crow?

We can see it as an invitation to weep over our brokenness. Our tears can be a reminder that the world is not as it should be. Yet in the tears, we can have hope that Jesus is alive and at work.

As Peter sat there weeping, I can imagine the words Jesus spoke years before rattling in his head:

God blesses those who mourn, for they will be comforted. (Matthew 5:4, NLT)

Jesus carried the burden of Peter's mess, just as he does for us all. And he does it because he doesn't want anyone left out.

💬 Questions to Ponder:

What do you think it was like for Peter to be questioned in the courtyard? Why do you think he denied knowing Jesus?

Have you ever been so overcome by fear that you acted in a way you regretted? What did you do when you "heard the rooster crow?"

How can you allow your sadness and tears over brokenness to lead you closer to Jesus rather than away from him?

What is one thing you learned about Jesus from this station?

Station V:
"What Is Truth?"

Station V of the Stations of the Cross: Jesus is judged by Pilate.
Bible Reading: John 18:28-19:16

Of all the characters in the Bible, I find Pontius Pilate one of the most fascinating.

He's a character familiar to most people, including those who've never read the Bible. I grew up attending Catholic Mass, where his name was mentioned every Sunday when reciting the Apostles Creed. (And, like every kid, I thought his name was Pontius *Pilot* and imagined a guy flying around in an airplane.)

I believe in Jesus Christ, his only Son, our Lord,
who was conceived by the Holy Spirit
and born of the virgin Mary.
He suffered under Pontius Pilate,
was crucified, died, and was buried.

Given how eager Pilate was to "wash his hands" of all responsibility, I'm not sure he would like to take credit for the suffering of Jesus.

Jesus' interaction with the Roman governor is our fifth stop along the Way of Sorrows. This fifth station is titled, "Jesus is judged by Pilate." But I wonder if a more accurate title might be, "Pilate is judged by the crowd."

After the Sanhedrin condemn Jesus, they bring him to the palace of

32

Pilate. They needed the Roman government's help to execute Jesus. Pilate, as governor, had this power.

Imagining the Person Pilate Was

It's a lengthy passage, but I encourage you to read the full exchange between Pilate and Jesus in John 18:28-19:16. As you do, try to imagine the kind of person Pilate was. What does he look like? How does he talk? How does he move about his palace?

I imagine Pilate as a nervous, anxious person who wakes up every morning with the fear of being "found out."

Do you ever feel that way? I know I do. Sometimes I feel like a fraud. Maybe this is the day the people around me will find out I'm not as smart as they think I am.

There are times when we feel the pressure of someone looking over our shoulder. For Pilate, the person breathing down his neck was a god among men—Caesar himself.

I imagine Pilate frantically pacing the halls of his palace as he tries to decide what to make of Jesus. Maybe he was a nail biter.

The Religious Leaders Wanted an Open-and-Shut Case

When the religious leaders brought Jesus to Pilate, they were not expecting much pushback. When Pilate asks what the charges are against Jesus, they become agitated:

"We wouldn't have handed him over to you if he weren't a criminal!" they retorted. (John 18:30, NLT)

There's not much funny about this story, but I find their answer humorous. Can you imagine a prosecutor making that kind of opening statement on day one of a trial?

"Look, we wouldn't be having a trial if the defendant weren't a criminal. So just forget all the evidence and witnesses and find him guilty so we can get to happy hour on time!"

After that, Pilate tries to figure out why Jesus' own people want him dead. He frantically questions Jesus, trying to make sense of it all. The religious leaders say Jesus is claiming to be a king. That would be enough to stamp Jesus' death warrant since Caesar is the only king in this empire. But Pilate hesitates. He can sense it's not earthly power Jesus is seeking.

"What Is Truth?"

As their conversation continues, Pilate questions Jesus about being a king. During this exchange, Pilate utters one of the most profound statements in the Bible.

Pilate said, "So you are a king?"

Jesus responded, "You say I am a king. Actually, I was born and came into the world to testify to the truth. All who love the truth recognize that what I say is true."

"What is truth?" Pilate asked. Then he went out again to the people and told them, "He is not guilty of any crime. But you have a custom of asking me to release one prisoner each year at Passover. Would you like me to release this 'King of the Jews'?" (John 18:37-39. NLT)

"What is truth?"

When I study a Bible passage, I like to read it in different versions to get new perspectives on the text. I was curious to see how each one would phrase Pilate's question. Well, guess what? Those three words were the same in every translation I checked. From the New King James to The Message, Pilate's question is, "What is truth?"

I wish I could hear the tone of Pilate's voice when he said those words.

If I was an actor playing Pilate in a play, I'm not sure how I would deliver that line.

How do you imagine those words sounding as they tumble out of Pilate's mouth? Which word do you think he emphasized?

Some people think Pilate said it as a joke, commenting on the absurdity of the situation. (Francis Bacon coined the phrase "jesting Pilate" in his essay "Of Truth"[8].)

Others propose Pilate was asking a sincere philosophical question.

I think Pilate's true motives lie somewhere in the middle.

About ten years ago, I stumbled across the book *Telling the Truth: The Gospel as Tragedy, Comedy, and Fairy Tale* by Frederick Buechner. Buechner's portrayal of Pilate captured my imagination and added to my fascination of the character.

In the book, Buechner depicts Pilate as a chain smoker who reads the morning paper as he rides to his office in a limousine. When Pilate confronts Jesus with his question—"*What is truth?*"—Beuchner describes it this way:

He asks it half because he would give as much as even his life to hear the answer and half because he believes there is no answer and would give a good deal to hear that too because it would mean just one thing less to have to worry about. He says, "What is truth?" and by way of an answer, the man with the split lip doesn't say a blessed thing. Or else his not saying anything, that is the blessed thing. You could hear a pin drop in the big, high-ceilinged room with Tiberius grinning down from the wall like a pumpkin, that one cigarette a little unsteady between the procurator's yellowed fingertips.[9]

---

8 "Francis Bacon Quotes." *BrainyQuote*, www.brainyquote.com/quotes/francis_bacon _149870.

9 Buechner, Frederick. *Telling the Truth: the Gospel as Tragedy, Comedy, and Fairy Tale.* Harper & Row, 1977.

Buechner portrays Pilate as a man on the verge of a breakdown. Here he is, inches away from the answer to his question—the man with the split lip who claims to be God. But life would be easier for Pilate if he walks away. And that's what he did. Pilate was the man who walked away from truth.

Despite walking away from truth, he still felt uneasy about sentencing Jesus to death. Three times in this scene, Pilate tells the people he finds no fault in Jesus. But in the end, the religious leaders win by threatening to put Pilate on trial.

Then Pilate tried to release [Jesus], but the Jewish leaders shouted, "If you release this man, you are no 'friend of Caesar.' Anyone who declares himself a king is a rebel against Caesar." (John 19:12, NLT)

If Caesar found out Pilate released a man who claimed to be king, Pilate would be a dead man. So Pilate hands Jesus over to be crucified, but not before trying to have things both ways. Matthew captures the dramatic gesture Pilate uses to free himself of responsibility.

Pilate saw that he wasn't getting anywhere and that a riot was developing. So he sent for a bowl of water and washed his hands before the crowd, saying, "I am innocent of this man's blood. The responsibility is yours!" (Matthew 27:24, NLT)

The Little Pilate in Us All

If I seem sympathetic to Pilate, it's only because I can see myself in him. The Bible is not a book filled with "good guys" and "bad guys," but complex people like me and you. We can see a reflection of ourselves in all of them, especially the ones who get it wrong.

Pilate chose to turn his back on truth because it was too dangerous to face. Maybe he caught a glimpse of truth in Jesus' eyes, but then wished he could unsee it. The truth came with a cost Pilate was unwilling to pay. When the pressure mounted and the fear started rising, Pilate caved.

We all want the truth. But when we find it, what do we do with it?

Sometimes it can be dangerous to know what the right thing to do is. Sometimes acting on what we know is true can be costly. It's easier to turn our backs like Pilate and pretend we didn't see it.

Sometimes I'll feel that nudge from God asking me to do something. Or stop doing something. Or swallow my pride and say I'm sorry. Or talk to that person I'd prefer not to engage with. Or take a risk for the benefit of someone else.

When I come face to face with truth, I pray I have the courage to not turn my back on it.

🗨 Questions to Ponder:

When you read the exchange between Jesus and Pilate, how do you picture Pilate?

Can you relate to Pilate in any way? Is there any truth God is asking you to act on that would be easier to walk away from? Today, ask God for the courage to face it.

What is one thing you learned about Jesus from this station?

Station VI:
Who Do We Crown With Thorns?

Station VI of the Stations of the Cross: Jesus is scourged and crowned with thorns.
Bible Reading: Mark 15:15-20

And they clothed [Jesus] in a purple cloak, and twisting together a crown of thorns, they put it on him. And they began to salute him, "Hail, King of the Jews!" And they were striking his head with a reed and spitting on him and kneeling down in homage to him. (Mark 15:17-19, ESV)

It didn't happen often, but there were occasions in elementary school where other kids made fun of me. I have cerebral palsy, and it affects the way I walk. I remember one afternoon when my friend (who also had a disability) and I were standing in line outside the cafeteria. Two boys passed by and started mocking us. They began to mimic the way we walked, laughing to each other as they wobbled around.

Before you start feeling too bad for me, let me finish the story. My friend and I came up with a plan to mock them right back. We started pointing and laughing at them. (Don't ask me what we were making fun of them for. I have no clue. It wasn't a very well thought out plan.) I'm not sure if we achieved our goal, but I do know all four of us looked like fools that day.

Mocking others gets ugly fast. There is something about being mocked that hurts deeper than an insult. Mocking is personal. When you mock someone, you are taking something true about a person and using it to inflict pain on them. You are twisting a thread of truth into a grotesque caricature. When we get mocked, our amygdala gets triggered, and we want to mock right back.

Jesus knew what it was like to be mocked ruthlessly. Jesus getting scourged and crowned with thorns is our sixth stop along the Way of Sorrows. It marks a turning point in the story. He has been officially sentenced to be crucified, and now the horror begins.

The scourging was a typical Roman protocol for anyone sentenced to be crucified. It's brutal, but it was not an uncommon practice in ancient Rome. The intent was to wear a person down so much that they wouldn't be able to survive on a cross for long.

When the soldiers crown Jesus with thorns, however, they are taking things a step further. They are no longer acting according to protocol, but deciding to have some "fun" with Jesus.

Horrific, Unspeakable Torture

So Pilate, wishing to satisfy the crowd, released for them Barabbas, and having scourged Jesus, he delivered him to be crucified. (Mark 15:15, ESV)

Scourging is not simply a whipping. According to the footnotes in the ESV Bible, scourging "consist[ed] of a severe beating with a multi-lashed whip containing embedded pieces of bone and metal." The whip would dig into flesh upon impact and tear it off when pulled back.

Some victims would go into shock from the agony of scourging and die right there. They may be considered the "lucky ones" since crucifixion was next.

The Bible doesn't go into detail about the scourging because it didn't have to. Early readers knew the horror of what it entailed. I did some research on what doctors say it was like for Jesus at that moment. As I read about the graphic nature of scourging and the pain Jesus endured, I felt a weight of sadness wash over me. I had to stop reading. If I couldn't even handle words on a page, how would I react if I witnessed this event?

If I saw Jesus being scourged that day, I know I would have to look away. I would turn my face away from the one who never looks away from me. I'm not proud to say that. It calls to mind the prophecy of Isaiah in the Old Testament:

He was despised and rejected—
a man of sorrows, acquainted with deepest grief.
We turned our backs on him and looked the other way.
He was despised, and we did not care. (Isaiah 53:3, NLT)

I believe Jesus begins bearing the sins of the world at this moment of scourging. The nightmare doesn't end until he gives up his spirit on the cross.

Crowning the King With Thorns

After the scourging, the soldiers decide to have some fun with Jesus. About 600 of them surround him—the same number present for his arrest in the Garden of Gethsemane. Here's how The Message version puts it:

The soldiers took Jesus into the palace (called Praetorium) and called together the entire brigade. They dressed him up in purple and put a crown plaited from a thorn-bush on his head. Then they began their mockery: "Bravo, King of the Jews!" They banged on his head with a club, spit on him, and knelt down in mock worship. After they had had their fun, they took off the purple cape and put his own clothes back on him. Then they marched out to nail him to the cross. (Mark 15:16-20, MSG)

In Station V, Jesus told Pilate he had a kingdom, but his kingdom wasn't from this world. (John 18:36) The soldiers took Jesus' words (which were true) and created a caricature out of it.

Oh, this guy thinks he's a king, huh? Well, let's give him what he wants!

They twisted together long, sharp thorns and placed it on Jesus' head. As the thorns dug into his skin, it heightened the pain sensations throughout his whole body. Then the mocking began.

They dressed Jesus in a purple robe because it was the color of royalty. They bowed down to him, pretending to show respect. They spit in his face.

What made the soldiers take things to this level of scorn?

It could be they did it to appease the crowd. It was Passover, and the Roman authorities needed to keep chaos from breaking loose in the streets. Pilate and his brigade could see how much Jesus' own people wanted him dead. By playing up this drama, they were giving the people what they wanted.

I think there was also a level of mob mentality. Would one or two soldiers have taken things to this extreme? Maybe, but it's far less likely. When you are one in a crowd of 600, it's easier to lose your individual responsibility. It's not me who's mocking and spitting at Jesus. It's all of us. I can hide behind others because we're all doing it.

Who Do We Crown With Thorns?

We still give out crowns of thorns today. Take a look on social media, and you'll see crowns of thorns everywhere.

Do you know what I rarely see on Facebook? I rarely see someone frame an opposing view in a way that tries to understand the original post. It's usually presented as an ugly caricature. They'll take one piece of truth and mock it brutally.

I know I'm guilty of this. It's easier for me to poke holes in an opposing view than to defend my own. And let's face it—it's more fun,

41

too, especially on the Internet, where you're not having a one-on-one conversation. My insult is just one more in an endless thread of comments. I don't feel the weight of my words the way I would if I were talking in person.

Of course, it happens offline too. And when it does, it can have long-lasting consequences. When I mock someone, I put up a wall between us. I cut off a chance at real communication. I risk losing the relationship.

Do you know what I think is the opposite of mocking? *Listening.* If mocking someone is creating a caricature of them, listening is attempting to perceive them as they truly are. We all bring something unique to the table. I gain much more by listening to you than by mocking you.

What Do We Do When Others Crown Us?

Yes, we all give out crowns of thorns. But we also get crowned by others, and it hurts.

It hurts when we're vulnerable and people mock us for it.

It hurts when people take something true about us and twist it for their own purposes.

It hurts, and our instinct is to want to hurt back. That was my instinct that day in elementary school.

So what do we do?

We look at Jesus wearing the crown of thorns. We look at Jesus even though we want to look away. We look at his broken body and remember that he paid for our sins. And for all the sins done against us.

We look at the man who stayed silent and forgave his mockers.

No, this doesn't mean we stay in toxic relationships. It doesn't mean we allow ourselves to be abused. We don't remain silent in these situations. If you're trapped in a cycle of abuse, please tell someone.

But in other cases, silence may be the best solution.

When a co-worker makes a snide remark, we don't have to snap back.

We don't have to respond to every sarcastic comment on Facebook. *(This is a tough one for me.)*

We don't have to defend every single opinion we have all the time.

We can forgive people who mock us and respond in love because that's what Jesus did. He knows how it feels to be scorned. And we know one day, King Jesus will trade in his crown of thorns for real crowns.

Then I saw heaven opened, and a white horse was standing there. Its rider was named Faithful and True, for he judges fairly and wages a righteous war. His eyes were like flames of fire, **and on his head were many crowns.** *A name was written on him that no one understood except himself. He wore a robe dipped in blood, and his title was the Word of God. The armies of heaven, dressed in the finest of pure white linen, followed him on white horses.* (Revelation 19:11-13, NLT, emphasis mine)

I'll never understand the agony Jesus went through as he began his journey to the cross. But knowing the shame he endured, I pray for the strength to stop handing out crowns of thorns to others.

💬 Questions to Ponder:

What do you think of the idea that mockery is "twisting a thread of truth into a grotesque caricature?" Have you ever been mocked in this way? How did it make you feel?

How can you choose to listen to someone when you feel like mocking them? How can you choose forgiveness when you get mocked by others?

What is one thing you learned about Jesus from this station?

Station VII:
Jesus vs. Skull Hill

**Station VII of the Stations of the Cross: Jesus takes up his cross.
Bible Reading: John 19:16-17, Mark 8:31-38**

So they took Jesus away. Carrying the cross by himself, he went to the place called Place of the Skull. (John 19:16-17, NLT)

When the COVID-19 pandemic hit us in early 2020, I found it hard to focus on much of anything. The days spent in lockdown had a surreal quality to them, and the nights were filled with an eerie restlessness. Every day we woke up to more bad news. During times like these, it's easy to look up to the heavens and wonder, "Why?"

Jesus' followers have been wrestling with the question of suffering for centuries. I don't want to offer simple, pat answers to it. But the journey down the *Via Dolorosa* reminds us that while suffering is real, Jesus is in it *with* us. He doesn't ask anything of us that he isn't willing to go through too.

Jesus taking up his cross is our seventh stop along the Way of Sorrows. After Jesus is scourged and mocked, he is forced to carry his cross to the site of his crucifixion. As he began his trek through the streets of Jerusalem with onlookers gawking, no one knew an epic battle was about to take place.

The Skull

Jesus was executed on Golgotha, which means "skull" in Aramaic. Golgotha was a skull-shaped hill just outside the walls of Jerusalem.[10] It's a grim image—a skull is a symbol of death. Jesus was marching toward a place no one returns from.

As an added cruelty, Jesus was forced to carry the instrument of his death. Most scholars agree that Jesus did not carry the entire cross, but the horizontal plank of wood. Author Ty Benbow explains the typical protocol of Roman executions:

As one approached such an awful and public death, the victim would often be ordered to carry the horizontal crossbeam known as the patibulum to the site of death. At the site of the execution, the crossbeam would be connected to the upright beam of the cross, and the victim would be nailed to the structure prior to the crucifix being hoisted upward.[11]

But Jesus wasn't just carrying a beam of wood that day. He was shouldering the sufferings of the world—all our tears, all our grief, all our pain. All the things in the world that don't make sense. Jesus was carrying the burden of every life that got cut short, and every senseless act of violence. And he was doing so willingly.

Following Jesus Down the Road of Suffering

As the disciples hid in the crowd, watching their friend suffer, they must have been confused. This was not the ending they had in mind. They thought Jesus was unstoppable. They had dreams and plans that didn't include a cross.

---

10   "Golgotha." Encyclopædia Britannica, Encyclopædia Britannica, Inc., www.britanni ca.com/place/Golgotha.

11   Benbow, Ty. Who Really Carried the Cross of Jesus?, 30 July 2013, answersingenes is.org/contradictions-in-the-bible/who-really-carried-the-cross-of-jesus/.

But they shouldn't have been confused at all. Jesus told them this day was coming.

One day while walking through a village, Jesus asked his disciples who they thought he was. Peter, always eager to be the first to answer, blurted out, "You are the Messiah" (Mark 8:29, NLT).

Peter got it right! He recognized Jesus as the promised one Israel had been waiting for. Jesus used this opportunity to talk openly with his friends. He was clear about the horror to come:

Then Jesus began to tell them that the Son of Man must suffer many terrible things and be rejected by the elders, the leading priests, and the teachers of religious law. He would be killed, but three days later he would rise from the dead. As he talked about this openly with his disciples, Peter took him aside and began to reprimand him for saying such things. (Mark 8:31-32, NLT)

It took some gall for Peter to "reprimand Jesus," but I get where he was coming from. Jesus admitted to being the Messiah, and Messiahs have ultimate power, right? They shouldn't have to suffer.

Things got worse for the disciples when Jesus dropped another truth bomb: They would have to join in on the suffering.

Then, calling the crowd to join his disciples, he said, "If any of you wants to be my follower, you must give up your own way, take up your cross, and follow me." (Mark 8:34, NLT)

Jesus was speaking to anyone who wanted to follow him. If I'm a follower of Jesus, then there's a cross with my name on it.

I'm sure Peter loved that one!

Suffering didn't make sense in Peter's worldview, just as it doesn't make sense to us.

Peter had to be thinking, *We're following the one true God. We believe all the right things. We're doing amazing things for God. Why do we have to make suffering part of the plan?*

I can't say I blame Peter for his aversion to suffering. I have it, too. I'm doing my best to follow Jesus and live the right way. Why do suffering and pain have to be part of the deal?

Because suffering is the path Jesus chose. He didn't run from it. He embraced it.

Yes, Jesus asks us to pick up our cross. But then he picks up his cross and leads the way.

I love the way The Message phrases Jesus' words about suffering:

Calling the crowd to join his disciples, he said, "Anyone who intends to come with me has to let me lead. **You're not in the driver's seat; I am. Don't run from suffering; embrace it.** *Follow me and I'll show you how. Self-help is no help at all. Self-sacrifice is the way, my way, to saving yourself, your true self. What good would it do to get everything you want and lose you, the real you? What could you ever trade your soul for?* (Mark 8:34-37, MSG, emphasis mine)

Who Won the Battle at Skull Hill?

Can I be honest with you?

On most days, I don't feel strong enough to carry my own cross. Sometimes the sadness of the world is too much to bear, and I buckle under the weight of it all.

What do we do when we're not strong enough to carry our cross?

We remember we're not in the driver's seat. Jesus is. And he is strong enough to carry our crosses when we can't.

I can't wrap my mind around the sadness of this world. I can't comprehend it. But I know God chose to do something about it. When

48

God saw the brokenness of this world, he decided to enter into it and do battle with it. As Jesus carried his cross toward Skull Hill, he was taking our sufferings with him.

So who won the battle?

As Jesus was hoisted on the cross, it looked like the Skull won. And there are days when it feels like the Skull is still winning.

The day after they buried Jesus, silence filled the earth. All the good he did, all the love he shared… It all seemed like it was for nothing. The Skull—death—had silenced the Sufferer.

But the Skull was proud and claimed victory too soon. Because a day later, Jesus—The Comeback Kid—made the ultimate comeback. He dealt death a knockout punch right in the jaw.

So in our sadness and suffering, let us have hope.

I can't help but feel like the Skull continues to claim victory a bit too soon.

🗨 Questions to Ponder:

Why do you think Jesus chose to achieve victory through the path of suffering?

What sadness or grief are you dealing with right now? As you think about Jesus carrying his cross, try to imagine that grief tacked onto it.

What cross is Jesus asking you to carry? How can you lean on Jesus when you are too weak to carry it?

What is one thing you learned about Jesus from this station?

Station VIII:
Simon the Mystery Man

Station VIII of the Stations of the Cross: Jesus is helped by Simon of Cyrene to carry his cross.
Bible Reading: Matthew 27:32, Mark 15:21, Luke 23:26

A passerby named Simon, who was from Cyrene, was coming in from the countryside just then, and the soldiers forced him to carry Jesus' cross. (Simon was the father of Alexander and Rufus.) (Mark 15:21, NLT)

When I'm reading the Bible, it's amazing how often I breeze past small details to get to the "good stuff." As we've been journeying to the cross with Jesus, I've encountered scenes familiar to me. Jesus' prayer in the Garden of Gethsemane. Judas' betrayal. The trial before Pilate. When I think of the symphony that is Easter, these are the "movements" I'm used to hearing.

I've never given much thought to the man who helped Jesus carry his cross—Simon of Cyrene. And yet, he is part of the Easter story as much as any of the other characters are. Simon's chance encounter with Jesus is our eighth stop along the Way of Sorrows.

Precious Little Ink Spilled on Simon

One reason it's easy to overlook Simon is because of how little space the gospel writers devote to his story. Matthew, Mark, and Luke all mention him, but only give him one verse each. Who is this mysterious man who was forced to carry Jesus' cross?

Mark packs in the most details about Simon. I find this interesting because Mark is the shortest gospel. His gospel is action-packed, moving quickly from scene to scene. If Mark provides any details about an event, I think it's worth stopping and paying attention.

I'm going to take a cue from every pastor in America and look at three things Mark's passage reveals about our mystery man. *(Three is the magic number in sermons, right?)*

1. Simon Was an Outsider

Simon, who was from Cyrene, was coming in from the countryside. (Mark 15:21, NLT)

Cyrene was located in modern-day Libya.[12]

This doesn't necessarily mean Simon was an outsider to the Jewish faith. He may have been a Jewish man whose family was dispersed to Libya, and now Simon was returning to celebrate the Passover. Or he may have been an African man who chose to follow Yahweh. Either way, there's a good chance this was Simon's first time visiting Jerusalem.

If that's the case, Simon has no context for what's happening. He's an outsider to all that is taking place. He hasn't been around to see all the events leading up to this moment. I can't imagine how Simon must have felt when he was thrown headfirst into this mess.

It's interesting. Throughout Jesus' ministry, he met with outsiders and left them changed. He met with Zacchaeus, the dishonest tax man, and filled him with joy (Luke 19:1-10). He met with a despised Samaritan woman and freed her of shame and guilt (John 4:1-42). Now, on the road to his own death, Jesus meets Simon, another outsider. Was Simon changed by this encounter? I think we'll see he was.

---

12 "What Do We Know about Simon of Cyrene?" CompellingTruth.org, www.compellin gtruth.org/Simon-of-Cyrene.html.

I can't help but notice a parallel between this story and the walk to Emmaus (Luke 24:13-35). In that story, Jesus meets two of his followers after resurrecting from the grave. They don't recognize Jesus and believe him to be a total stranger. They feel defeated that their friend has just been crucified. As they walk along the road to Emmaus, Jesus explains why everything had to happen the way it did.

As Jesus walked to his death with Simon following, I wonder what words Jesus spoke to him.

Jesus' words always left outsiders changed. And they still do.

2. Simon Was Forced to Carry Jesus' Cross

All three gospel writers make it clear that Simon didn't volunteer for the job of carrying Jesus' cross. Luke says the soldiers "grabbed Simon." (Luke 23:26, CEB) It sounds like it was done out of haste.

Remember, Jesus started out carrying his cross (Station VII). As he reached the city entrance, he must have collapsed out of sheer exhaustion. The soldiers were on a schedule and grabbed Simon out of frustration to keep things moving along.

Some commentators make Simon out to be a saint and say he carried the cross willingly. Others portray him as doing it begrudgingly. I don't think we can know what Simon's attitude was. Maybe the real question is, what would *we* do if we were in Simon's shoes? I can tell you, I wouldn't be too happy if I were grabbed and forced to carry a criminal's cross.

How do we handle disruptions? Disruptions aren't fun. They prevent us from doing the things we want to do. But every disruption is an opportunity to serve others. Ironically, Jesus told us what to do when we find ourselves in Simon's situation:

If anyone forces you to go one mile, go with them two miles. (Matthew 5:41, NIV)

When I'm faced with a situation I'd rather avoid, I pray for the strength to go above and beyond what is expected of me.

3. Simon's Story Didn't End That Day

Mark includes a detail about Simon that Matthew and Luke do not.

Simon was the father of Alexander and Rufus.

It seems like such a throwaway piece of information. Why tell us the names of Simon's kids?

If Mark took the time to include this detail, it means he expected his readers to know who Alexander and Rufus were. He was doubling down on his story and saying, *If you don't believe me, go ask Alexander and Rufus. They'll tell you the story from their father's perspective.*

When the Apostle Paul closes out his letter to the Romans, he includes this greeting:

*Greet **Rufus**, chosen in the Lord, and his mother, who has been a mother to me, too.* (Romans 16:13, NIV, emphasis mine)

True, there's no way of knowing if the Rufus Paul is referring to is the son of Simon. But again, why would Mark include this detail?

There's a good chance Simon was changed the day he was forced to carry Jesus' cross. I don't think he was happy about it, but as he saw this innocent man get crucified, something changed. And when he got word a few days later that Jesus was alive, it set him on a different course. A new story began for Simon the day he carried Jesus' cross.

There's still a lot of mystery surrounding Simon of Cyrene. I wish we knew more about him. I'd love to ask him his thoughts about the whole event.

Looking back, would he consider it an honor to carry the cross of Jesus?

And looking forward, will we?

🗨 Questions to Ponder:

Which detail of Simon's story do you find most interesting? What other information can you gather about Simon from the little written about him?

What crosses do you have the opportunity to carry this week? What is your attitude about it?

What is one thing you learned about Jesus from this station?

Station IX:
Weeping With the Daughters of Jerusalem

Station IX of the Stations of the Cross: Jesus meets the women of Jerusalem.
Bible Reading: Luke 23:27-31, Luke 19:41-44

If you have a close relationship with someone, you're not going to like everything they have to say. Words from a good friend can encourage you. But they can often challenge you, and sometimes leave you with a feeling of uneasiness.

The same goes for when Jesus speaks to us. When I am feeling tired and discouraged, I take comfort in these words:

Then Jesus said, "Come to me, all of you who are weary and carry heavy burdens, and I will give you rest." (Matthew 11:28, NLT)

Is there anyone who *doesn't* like hearing those words?

There are other times when Jesus challenges me with his words:

"You have heard the law that says, 'Love your neighbor' and hate your enemy. But I say, love your enemies! Pray for those who persecute you!" (Matthew 5:43-44, NLT)

Sometimes I forget loving your enemies is a command from Jesus, not a friendly suggestion. But as uncomfortable as it makes me, at least it's clear. I know what it means. (Which is why I have such a hard time doing it!)

But then there are times when Jesus' words aren't just uncomfortable. They're chilling. They fill me with uneasiness and make me want to flip my Bible back to the "I will give you rest" part. One of these times is when Jesus gives an ominous warning to the daughters of Jerusalem.

Jesus' meeting with the women of Jerusalem is our ninth stop along the Way of Sorrows. As Jesus continues his journey toward Skull Hill, with Simon carrying his cross, he stops to have a solemn conversation with women in mourning.

This is a tough passage of Scripture and one I can't pretend to understand fully. In my research, I've found varying opinions on what these verses mean. As I add mine to the mix, I want to tread carefully and acknowledge I don't have all the answers.

Where Did All the Men Go?

A large crowd trailed behind, including many grief-stricken women. (Luke 23:27, NLT)

As Jesus marches to his death, Luke tells us a large crowd follows him. No doubt, this crowd is filled with scoffers and mockers. But you also have this group of women who are heartbroken about what is happening.

Where did the twelve disciples go? They scattered and ran during Jesus' arrest. Maybe some are hidden in the crowd. (We know that at least John was present at the crucifixion.) If the rest are around, they remain silent. But not these women. They let out their anguish as they see their friend suffering.

I think this is remarkable. In a time and culture that undervalues women, the gospels portray them as heroes. The women are the ones who go to the tomb on the third day (Luke 24:1-12). The women are the ones who are told by an angel that Jesus is alive. And the women are the ones who get the first job of sharing the good news. (And the men didn't believe it, by the way.)

In the Easter story, the disciples are portrayed as fools. The women are depicted as faithful.

Who Were the "Daughters of Jerusalem"?

When I read this passage, I usually imagine a small group of three or four women. Maybe the most famous ones—you know, maybe Martha and all the Marys.

But Luke said there were "many" women. Jesus was a friend to women. He valued them. I'm sure there were many women in that group who he met throughout his three-year ministry. And maybe more who didn't know him personally but had seen the healings and heard the stories. They were sad that this is how Jesus' life had to end.

When Jesus sees them mourning, he stops to speak to them. And now we get to the words that bring a sense of uneasiness:

But Jesus turned and said to them, "Daughters of Jerusalem, don't weep for me, but weep for yourselves and for your children. For the days are coming when they will say, 'Fortunate indeed are the women who are childless, the wombs that have not borne a child and the breasts that have never nursed.' People will beg the mountains, 'Fall on us,' and plead with the hills, 'Bury us.' For if these things are done when the tree is green, what will happen when it is dry?" (Luke 23:28-31, NLT)

These are haunting words that seem to be void of compassion. It sounds like Jesus is saying, "Hey, if you think what I'm going through looks bad, wait until you see what's coming around the corner for you!"

I read one commentator who says Jesus was scolding the women. Ouch!

I don't think that's the case. Jesus didn't brush the women aside. He took time out of his own suffering to respond to them. He was entrusting these faithful women with one of his final teachings. Father Jerome Kodell says:

Surely part of the reason these women walk with this suffering prophet is because they sense that their own lives would be affected by the disturbing events underway. Jesus' words do not sound like comfort... But they serve to focus the vague uneasiness of the women, **and, in a society that disregards the concerns of women as imaginary or emotional, Jesus comforts them by taking them seriously.**[13]

The daughters of Jerusalem understood suffering more than most in the crowd that day. Jesus knew they could handle his words of warning.

No One Is Immune to Suffering

So, what was Jesus' warning about?

Most scholars agree Jesus, at least in part, is prophesying the fall of Jerusalem. About 40 years after his death, Roman armies overtook the city of Jerusalem and destroyed it.

The violence was brutal. Mothers watched their children die. In some cases, the food supply was cut, and children starved to death. Those were days when, as Jesus says, the fortunate women were the childless ones.

The fall of Jerusalem was an event to weep over. But I think Jesus is also alluding to something more. I believe Jesus is lamenting all human suffering. The suffering not tied to one single event. The everyday pain these women knew so well. Jesus ends his lament with this metaphor:

For if these things are done when the tree is green, what will happen when it is dry? (Luke 23:31, NLT)

---

13   Kodell, Jerome. "Jesus Meets the Women of Jerusalem." *Catholic Diocese of Little Rock*, www.dolr.org/stations-of-the-cross/eighth-station.

Jesus is the green tree, full of life and goodness. Jesus is saying if worldly powers are doing all these things to him, then none of the other trees are safe, either. If Jesus had to endure suffering, then no one is immune.

But it also means that no one is immune to *causing* suffering, either. We are part of the problem. *I* am part of the problem.

When God came into this world as a human, we rejected him. We mocked him and cheered as he was hung on the cross and left to die.

No, we weren't there on the day it happened. But we still reject Jesus in our daily lives. We don't love the way he loved. We hurt people. We leave people out. We commit all kinds of atrocities and horrors against other humans.

And so even as we endure suffering, we also cause suffering in others.

The Way to Peace

As I said before, Jesus' words are chilling. This whole passage leaves us with a sense of dread. A group of women mourn Jesus' suffering, and in response, he grieves for the world's suffering.

Is there any hope?

With Jesus, there is always hope, because Easter is coming.

About a week before he was crucified—on Palm Sunday—Jesus rode into Jerusalem on a humble colt. As he entered the city, he wept for it, just as he told the daughters of Jerusalem to do.

But as he came closer to Jerusalem and saw the city ahead, he began to weep. "How I wish today that you of all people would understand the way to peace. But now it is too late, and peace is hidden from your eyes." (Luke 19:41-42, NLT)

Jesus was weeping because the people had rejected the way to peace. And what is the way to peace? It's through Jesus.

Even though the people rejected him, he wasn't rejecting them. He continued his journey to the cross to make a way to peace for us. He was making a way to peace for the daughters of Jerusalem, who knew suffering. He was making a way to peace for us, who know (and cause) suffering.

Jesus told the women to weep, but not forever. At the cross, Jesus was giving sorrow a deadline.

We await the day Jesus will return. He will "wipe every tear from [our] eyes, and there will be no more death or sorrow or crying or pain. All these things are gone forever" (Revelation 21:4, NLT).

Until that day, it is not only okay—but right—to weep with the daughters of Jerusalem. But as we do, we remember the hope contained in our tears.

🗨 Questions to Ponder:

How do you interpret the words Jesus spoke to the daughters of Jerusalem?

What suffering have you endured in life? What suffering have your actions brought on others? Take some time to mourn for both today.

What is one thing you learned about Jesus from this station?

Station X:
The Miracle of Staying on the Cross

Station X of the Stations of the Cross: Jesus is crucified.
Bible Reading: Mark 15:23-32

As I write this, it is raining outside. It's a dark and gloomy day, which is appropriate for the final stretch down the *Via Dolorosa*. The light of Easter is coming, but before we get there, things are going to get darker. Jesus being crucified is our tenth stop along the Way of Sorrows.

Jesus has been arrested, beaten, mocked, and sentenced to death in less than a day. Now, at nine in the morning (no more than twelve hours since his prayer in Gethsemane), he is crucified.

Pilate's Jab at the Religious Leaders

As the soldiers nail Jesus to the cross, they put a sign next to him:

A sign announced the charge against him. It read, "The King of the Jews." (Mark 15:26, NLT)

Mark doesn't tell us anything more about this. But if we flip over to John's gospel, we get an interesting piece of added information. The phrasing on the sign irked the religious leaders. They go to Pilate and tell him to change it.

Then the leading priests objected and said to Pilate, "Change it from 'The King of the Jews' to 'He said, I am King of the Jews.'" (John 19:21, NLT)

The religious leaders want it to be clear that they don't see Jesus as their king. He's being crucified because he *claimed* to be king.

Pilate is not in the mood to do these men any more favors. He has been their puppet all night, and now he gives one quick jab to their egos.

Pilate replied, "No, what I have written, I have written." (John 19:22, NLT)

We have already seen in Station V how passive Pilate is. I can imagine him shrugging his shoulders as he says this, washing his hands of responsibility again. This time, though, he probably took some pleasure in not caving to their demand.

What Will It Take to Believe Jesus?

As Jesus is being crucified, the religious leaders begin mocking him:

The leading priests and teachers of religious law also mocked Jesus. "He saved others," they scoffed, "but he can't save himself! Let this Messiah, this King of Israel, come down from the cross so we can see it and believe him!" Even the men who were crucified with Jesus ridiculed him. (Mark 15:31-32, NLT)

This passage is dripping with irony. The religious leaders want Jesus to save himself. If he comes down from the cross, then they'll believe.

But these men have already seen Jesus do amazing things. They've seen the healings. (And admit to it when they say, "He saved others.") They've heard the wisdom of Jesus' teachings. And yet they still do not believe.

If Jesus crawls down from the cross, will that be the game-changer that persuades them? I don't think so. Three days later, when Jesus rises from the grave, most of these men still won't believe.

Seeing isn't always believing. Sometimes we look for signs, but we really don't want them. We're just looking for a way to delay doing what we already know is right.

As I thought about this, it led me to ponder an interesting question.

What would be a bigger miracle for Jesus—for him to get down from the cross, or to stay on it?

In Mark 2, Jesus heals a paralyzed man. But that's not the real miracle. The real miracle is he forgives the man of his sins. When the religious leaders accuse Jesus of blasphemy, Jesus performs a lesser miracle (the healing) to prove the bigger miracle. Jesus tells them:

Is it easier to say to the paralyzed man 'Your sins are forgiven,' or 'Stand up, pick up your mat, and walk'? So I will prove to you that the Son of Man has the authority on earth to forgive sins." Then Jesus turned to the paralyzed man and said, "Stand up, pick up your mat, and go home!" (Mark 2:9-11, NLT)

The Real Miracle

While Jesus was on the cross, the priests and teachers were asking him to perform a lesser miracle.

It would have been easy for Jesus to skip over the cross. It's what Satan tried to get him to do (Matthew 4:8-11). It's what Peter wanted him to do (Mark 8:31-33). And during his arrest, there were thousands of angels standing by, ready to whisk him away from danger at his command (Matthew 26:53). The real miracle occurred when Jesus *chose* the path of suffering to redeem us.

Even as these men were mocking Jesus, they were witnessing a miracle. They were staring at a man who was choosing love instead of hate. They were mocking a man who was paying the price for their cruelty at that very moment. And he was doing so willingly.

When life looks gloomy, I want to remember the miracle of Jesus staying put on the cross. It would have been far easier to show off his power and come down. It was the miracle that set messy, broken humans free from their sin.

It was the most horrific yet life-giving miracle ever accomplished.

> ### 💬 Questions to Ponder:
>
> Have you ever looked for a sign from God, even though you really didn't want one? What were you trying to delay doing?
>
> Why do you think Jesus chose to stay on the cross when he could have unleashed his power anytime? What does the miracle of Jesus staying on the cross mean to you?
>
> What is one thing you learned about Jesus from this station?

Station XI:
Thief for Hire

Station XI of the Stations of the Cross: Jesus promises his kingdom to the repentant thief.
Bible Reading: Luke 23:39-43, Matthew 20:1-15

During Jesus' time on earth, he loved to tell stories. We call these stories parables because in each one, Jesus reveals something about how God and his kingdom work.

But Jesus didn't just tell stories. He lived them out. I am convinced that for every parable Jesus told, there was a true story that punctuated it.

Jesus told the Parable of the Prodigal Son (Luke 15:11-32) to help people understand nobody is too far gone to come home to God. Then he welcomed the tax collector Zacchaeus home (Luke 19:1-10).

Jesus told the Parable of the Sower (Matthew 13:1-23) to explain why some people would reject him. Then he met a rich man who walked away from him because the lure of wealth was calling (Mark 10:17-27). The man was like the seed that fell among the thorns in Jesus' story.

Now, while dying on the cross, Jesus is about to bring another one of his parables to life. Jesus' interaction with the repentant thief is our eleventh stop along the Way of Sorrows.

Jesus is crucified between two criminals. One criminal mocks Jesus, but the other one senses something significant happening. This man (often called the "repentant thief" or "good thief" in Christian tradition) begs Jesus for mercy.

Then [the criminal] said, "Jesus, remember me when you come into your kingdom." Jesus answered him, "Truly I tell you, today you will be with me in paradise." (Luke 23:42-43, NIV)

Why Did Jesus Give This Criminal a Hall Pass?

I remember being in school and having to ask the teacher for a pass to go to the bathroom. The worst time to ask for a pass was when you just got caught participating in some shenanigans. You weren't going anywhere.

This criminal was up to shenanigans his whole life. And now, moments before his death, he wants to get on board with what Jesus is doing? After years of doing life his way, he's finally ready to submit to Jesus? How convenient when there's not much of a future left for him.

Isn't it too little, too late?

Not to Jesus. As Jesus hangs there with outstretched arms, he welcomes the criminal home. This must have been shocking to anyone watching. But it shouldn't have been a surprise, because Jesus already told a story about this criminal.

Getting Paid a Full Wage for an Hour's Work

In Matthew 20, Jesus tells a parable about the manager of a vineyard who goes out to hire some workers. He hires workers early in the morning, and they agree on a price.

Later in the morning, the vineyard manager sees some more people in need of work. So he hires them, promising to pay a fair wage.

This happens several times throughout the day. Each time the manager goes out, he sees more people in need of work, and he brings them into the vineyard. Toward the end of the day, the manager still sees more people who need work. At this point, he wonders why they are standing around not doing anything.

At five o'clock he went back and found still others standing around. He said, "Why are you standing around all day doing nothing?" They said, "Because no one hired us." (Matthew 20:6-7, MSG)

No one hired them. The people standing around wanted to work—they wanted to be included—but no one invited them in. They were left out.

Do we know anyone standing around, feeling left out? How can we invite them into something bigger?

At the end of the workday, the vineyard manager pays all the people he hired. But in an unexpected twist, he pays everyone the same amount of money.

For the workers who worked all day, this is a travesty of justice. They complain about getting paid the same amount as the workers who only worked an hour.

Now—this is important—the workers who worked all day weren't paid *less* than the wage they agreed on. They received what they were promised. But when they saw everyone else get paid the same, it bothered them.

The vineyard manager replies to this complaint pragmatically.

He replied to the one speaking for the rest, "Friend, I haven't been unfair. We agreed on the wage of a dollar, didn't we? So take it and go. I decided to give to the one who came last the same as you. Can't I do what I want with my own money? Are you going to get stingy because I am generous?" (Matthew 20:13-15, MSG)

Shouldn't the response to generosity always be joy? Why do we get so bent out of shape when we see someone get a gift we don't think they deserve?

Thief for Hire

Back to the criminal on the cross. How do we feel about this thief who was welcomed into the vineyard as the sun was setting?

Do we resent him for being forgiven and welcomed by Jesus? Or do we celebrate the generosity of God?

I don't know this man's story. I don't know what led him into a life of crime. But I'm guessing he lived a lonely life. A hard life. I'm guessing no one took the chance to invite him into a bigger story. Nobody stopped to show him compassion. After all, why would a criminal deserve compassion?

For all us workers who were hired early in the morning, we should clap and cheer for the workers who came in at dusk. As author J. Ellsworth Kalas says in his book *Parables from the Back Side*:

I was fortunate—so magnificently fortunate!—to become a Christian when I was not quite eleven years old. I was hired early in the morning, at the beginning of life's day. So it is that I have been blessed through all my life with a sense of life's purpose, value, and beauty. How dare I, then, be bitter about those who have waited all day in the marketplace, if at the end of the journey they are blessed with an eternity as good as mine? When I stand before the Great Landowner as he passes out the silver pieces of eternity, I might well take mine and say, "Give part of this to that poor soul who didn't come to faith in Christ until he was sixty years old . . . and to that woman who became a believer only when she was dying… Give them part of my reward, because they stood in the marketplace for so long, because no one hired them, while my life was filled with purpose."[14]

If we've been working in the vineyard for a while, let's go out and invite others. And then let's celebrate when they get paid a wage they don't deserve. Because if we stop to consider it, we don't deserve our wage, either.

---

14   Kalas, J. Ellsworth. *Parables from the Back Side: Bible Stories with a Twist.* Abingdon Press, 1992.

And for those who are still standing around, we welcome you. The sun hasn't set yet! It's not too late to come into the vineyard. God doesn't want anyone left out, and it wouldn't be the same without you here!

💬 Questions to Ponder:

Why do you think, while hanging on a cross, the criminal recognized Jesus as a king?

If you are a follower of Jesus, what "hour of the day" were you hired? How do you feel about those who were hired later than you?

Do you know anyone who is standing around, waiting to be hired? How can you invite them into the bigger story of God?

What is one thing you learned about Jesus from this station?

Station XII:
A Family Defined by Love

Station XII of the Stations of the Cross: Jesus entrusts Mary and John to each other.
Bible Reading: John 19:25-27

In the summer of 2019, I joined a team traveling to Malawi, Africa. We partnered with a wonderful organization called Children of the Nations (COTN). They were hosting a camp for children with disabilities, and we went to learn and support them in whatever way we could.

One of the translators at COTN was a young man named Allan. He, along with several other translators, guided us on our adventures for two weeks.

From the moment I arrived in Malawi to the moment I left, Allan was by my side. There were days we had to walk long distances, which was a challenge because of my cerebral palsy. Allan gave me an arm to lean on. He helped me stumble through rough terrain and up steep hills. And he did it all with joy.

Allan treated me like family, even though we just met. Why? Because to Allan, we *were* family. We had a bond that ran thicker than blood. It was the bond that comes from being part of the family of God—a family that traces its roots all the way back to the cross.

Jesus used his final breaths of life to begin forming this family. His call to entrust Mary and John to each other is our twelfth stop along the Way of Sorrows.

Squeezing Every Ounce Out of Life

I find it amazing how Jesus was still loving and serving people while hanging from the cross. Even while enduring agony, Jesus was living a life of purpose. He was in full control of his surroundings.

Sometimes Jesus is portrayed as a helpless victim on the cross, taking abuse from an angry father (God). But this isn't the Jesus we meet on the *Via Dolorosa*. Jesus chose the way of suffering to set his people free of the darkness oppressing them. Hebrews 12:2 gives us a glimpse into this willingness to take on the cross:

Because of the joy awaiting him, he endured the cross, disregarding its shame. (NLT)

While on the cross, Jesus continues to set things right by offering redemption to a thief, and then by creating the nucleus of a family of believers.

Standing near the cross were Jesus' mother, and his mother's sister, Mary (the wife of Clopas), and Mary Magdalene. When Jesus saw his mother standing there beside the disciple he loved, he said to her, "Dear woman, here is your son." And he said to this disciple, "Here is your mother." And from then on this disciple took her into his home. (John 19:25-27, NLT)

As Jesus looks down from the cross, he sees a bunch of Marys standing near him. As a side note, little details like this are why I take the Bible seriously. If I were making this story up, I would never name three different characters Mary. It's too confusing. Why are there so many women named Mary at the cross? Because there happened to be a lot of women named Mary at the cross!

There is some debate among scholars about how many women were in this group. Is there three or four? The question comes down to how you read that first sentence. Is the text saying Jesus' mother Mary had a sister also named Mary (who is the wife of Cleopas)? Or is Jesus' mother's sister a separate woman?

If thinking about that gives you a headache, don't worry. The main idea remains the same: Jesus is surrounded by faithful women at his death. And one of these women was Jesus' mother, Mary.

A Mother's Grief

It couldn't have been easy for Mary to watch her son die. In the back of her mind, she knew something like this was coming. When Jesus was a baby, Mary and Joseph went to the temple to dedicate him. There, they met a man named Simeon who gave Mary a stark warning:

"This child is destined to cause many in Israel to fall, and many others to rise. He has been sent as a sign from God, but many will oppose him. As a result, the deepest thoughts of many hearts will be revealed. And a sword will pierce your very soul." (Luke 2:34-35, NLT)

I'm sure every nail driven into Jesus' wrists was like a sword piercing through Mary's soul.

As Jesus sees Mary, he has compassion for her. She has been faithfully serving God by caring for and raising him. She loved this Son of God the best she knew how, even though it was confusing at times. (She also played the mother card once or twice and called in a special favor—see John 2:1-12!)

Jesus also sees John in the crowd. John is penning this story, and he likes referring to himself as "the disciple Jesus loved." I always thought that was a bit egotistical, but maybe it's not. John felt Jesus' love deeply. He experienced it on a personal level. That kind of connection to Jesus is available to all of us. We can all claim the title of "the person Jesus loves."

As Jesus is about to give up his life, he forms a new family between Mary and John. He tells Mary that John is her son. He tells John that Mary is his mother.

Caring for the Vulnerable

Why does Jesus bond Mary and John in this way?

Mary is probably a widow. The last time we read about Joseph, Jesus' earthly father, Jesus is still a boy (Luke 2:41-52). Joseph was significantly older than Mary and has passed away.

In the ancient Near East, widows were vulnerable. (They still are in many places.) They had few rights and were often exploited by religious leaders—the same people who were supposed to protect them under God's law.

Widows looked to their sons to provide them with protection and care. In Luke 7:11-17, Jesus meets a widow whose only son has died. Jesus' heart goes out to her. He feels terrible, but not simply because it's sad to lose a child. Jesus knows how much more difficult her life will be now. So he decides to help by bringing her son back to life!

Jesus had this same compassion for Mary. As her oldest son, it was his responsibility to look after her. Now that he's dying, it's time to come up with a contingency plan.

Mary had other sons. It would make sense for Jesus to entrust Mary to one of them. Right now, though, they're nowhere in sight. They think Jesus is crazy, but at least a couple of them (James and Jude) come around and start following Jesus later. *(I'm guessing when you see your brother walk out of a tomb, you finally stop ragging on him.)*

So Jesus gives John the responsibility of caring for Mary. John, who had his feet washed by Jesus twelve hours earlier. John, who has just heard Jesus give him a new commandment.

"Love each other. Just as I have loved you, you should love each other. Your love for one another will prove to the world that you are my disciples." (John 13:34-35, NLT)

73

Now John has a chance to live that out.

Mary has a job too. She has a new son in John. A son who will need wisdom and encouragement as this new thing called the "church" gets started.

By bonding Mary and John together, Jesus has created a family that will become the basis for a new community. This community will be marked by love and care for the most vulnerable.

A Family Defined by Love

For the two weeks I was in Malawi, Allan served me with compassion and love. Every time I stumbled, he caught me. Every time I needed something, he was there. And he did it with such joy.

On the day I left Malawi to come home, Allan said, "My brother, I will miss you so much."

Allan and I are brothers, not because of blood but because we both follow a man named Jesus. We're part of a family called the church. We're a family commanded by Jesus to be defined by love. Allan lived that out.

Are we living it out?

When John began caring for Mary, it must have looked crazy to the outside world. Why would he take responsibility for someone when it's not his job?

Does the love we have for each other look crazy to the outside world?

And, by extension, does that same love spill over to the outside world?

I pray it does, especially during challenging times.

✎ Questions to Ponder:

How many women do you think were standing by the cross? *(Just kidding! Unless you really want to answer it.)*

Have you ever been shown exceptional kindness by someone you just met? Why do you think they treated you that way?

Who has God entrusted you to care for? How can you serve them with joy in the days ahead?

What is one thing you learned about Jesus from this station?

Station XIII:
A Soldier's Story

**Station XIII of the Stations of the Cross: Jesus dies on the cross.
Bible Reading: Mark 15:33-39**

When the Roman officer who stood facing him saw how he had died, he exclaimed, "This man truly was the Son of God!" (Mark 15:39, NLT)

It has been a long, painful journey down the *Via Dolorosa* for Jesus. He has experienced abandonment, mockery, abuse, and torture. Now we see Jesus breathing his last breath. Jesus dying on the cross is our thirteenth stop along the Way of Sorrows.

Mark packs a lot of action into these seven verses. There is a lot that can be said about the strange events that unfold:

* The way creation reacted to Jesus on the cross by darkening itself for three hours (v. 33).

* The sad words Jesus cries from the cross: "My God, my God, why have you abandoned me?" (v. 34) Jesus is quoting Psalm 22, a psalm that foreshadows several of the events of the crucifixion. It begins in despair but ends in hope.

* The way the Temple curtain was torn in two at Jesus' final cry (v. 37-38). This curtain acted as a barrier to the Holy of Holies, the inner chamber of the Temple where God's presence dwelt. But it could no longer hold itself together under the weight of Jesus' sacrifice.

Entire books can be written about these topics, and by people way smarter than me. Today though, I find myself drawn to the Roman officer who marveled at Jesus after he died.

Just a Typical Day at Work

This officer (referred to as a *centurion* in most translations) had a front-row seat to Jesus' night of horror. A centurion was a commander, so he was in charge of the soldiers who handled Jesus. Did he join in with the mocking and beating of Jesus when the soldiers crowned him with thorns? Maybe. Or maybe he was too dignified for such games.

Maybe he was the one who ordered Simon of Cyrene to carry Jesus' cross. Once on Skull Hill, he may have been the one to give the order to drive the nails through Jesus' wrists and raise up the cross. Really, this was just another day at the office. His job was to oversee the crucifixion of criminals.

But somewhere along the line, Jesus stopped looking like an ordinary criminal to him. Maybe it was the way Jesus interacted with the powers of the world—he didn't beg for his life like other criminals did. Maybe it was the words of love he heard Jesus speak from the cross. Maybe it was the strange darkness covering the land. Or maybe Jesus had spoken words of truth to this officer as they traveled along the road.

Whatever it was, something stirred in this man's soul as he looked at Jesus' lifeless body. I imagine him staring up at the cross, mouth gaping, as he wraps words around his thoughts. "This man truly was the Son of God!"

Another soldier walks over to him. "What was that, sir? Hey, uh, should we take these bodies down now?"

"What? Uhh, yes. Yes, take them down," the centurion replies, trying to maintain his composure.

What a declaration for a Roman officer to make! If any of the religious leaders overheard him, they would have lost their minds.

Of course, the Roman officer was not the first person in the world to recognize Jesus as the Son of God. In Mark 8:29, Peter boldly declared that Jesus was the Messiah.

And after Jesus rose from the grave, many other people came to the same conclusion. When you see a dead man having breakfast on the beach with his friends, you begin to realize something is up!

But to recognize Jesus as the Son of God when he's just been killed and all hope is gone? This Roman officer may be the only person to have done such a thing.

So What Happened to the Roman Officer?

We don't know. I'm guessing he had a lot to think about in the days ahead, especially as the rumors started that Jesus was alive. Maybe he felt the weight of his actions against Jesus.

What we *do* know is that it wasn't too late for him. While on the cross, Jesus was paying the cost for this officer's sins. He was paving the way for this officer to be with God.

Like the Roman officer, I stand guilty. I wasn't at the cross that day, but if I had been, I would be no more innocent than anyone else there. As Stuart Townend wrote in the hymn "How Deep The Father's Love For Us:"

Behold the man upon a cross,
My sin upon his shoulders;
Ashamed, I hear my mocking voice
Call out among the scoffers.[15]

---

15 "How Deep the Father's Love." *Stuart Townend*, www.stuarttownend.co.uk/song /how-deep-the-fathers-love-for-us/.

Before rushing to the beauty of the resurrection, I want to marvel at Jesus' lifeless body the way the Roman officer did. As I consider my own brokenness, I pray for the humility to cry out, "This man truly is the Son of God!"

💬 Questions to Ponder:

Why do you think the Roman officer made such a bold declaration after Jesus died?

Take some time today to consider your own sin and brokenness and the cost Jesus was willing to pay for it.

What is one thing you learned about Jesus from this station?

Station XIV:
A Day of Darkness

Station XIV of the Stations of the Cross: Jesus is placed in the tomb.
Bible Reading: Matthew 27:57-61

Joseph took the body and wrapped it in a long sheet of clean linen cloth. He placed it in his own new tomb, which had been carved out of the rock. Then he rolled a great stone across the entrance and left. (Matthew 27:59-60, NLT)

"It's always darkest just before daylight breaks."

That's how the saying goes. But what if you don't know when daylight is coming, or even *if* it's coming? What if you are engulfed in darkness, and there is no light at the end of the tunnel? That's the situation Jesus' friends find themselves in after Jesus is taken off the cross and buried.

Jesus getting placed in the tomb is our fourteenth stop along the Way of Sorrows. Traditionally, this is the final stop of the Stations of the Cross. (But, as mentioned in the Introduction, I've also included a chapter on the resurrection of Jesus.) We've come to the end of the road, and it's an ending marked by, well... sorrow.

Honoring Jesus in Death

As the day drew to an end on Good Friday, a man named Joseph (from the town of Arimathea) asked Pilate for Jesus' body. He wanted to give it a proper burial.

Joseph was a secret follower of Jesus.[16] He was a member of the Sanhedrin—the group of religious leaders behind the plot to kill Jesus. This was the group of men who arrested Jesus under cover of night, held a phony trial, and then brutally beat him (Station III).

It makes me wonder if Joseph was present at that trial. Maybe he was and hovered in the corner, ashamed of what was taking place. Luke tells us Joseph "had not agreed with the decision and actions of the other religious leaders" (Luke 23:51). But we don't know how vocal he was about his reservations. We do know he kept his devotion to Jesus a secret because he was afraid of these powerful men (John 19:38).

I cannot judge Joseph for this. How often have I kept my devotion to Jesus a secret? How often do I stay quiet out of fear of being ridiculed? The Sanhedrin was not a group you wanted mad at you. Intimidation was their game. And if you were part of their group and betrayed them, that made the situation even stickier.

But now Joseph boldly goes to Pilate and asks for Jesus' body to be released to his care. Maybe he felt like this was the least he could do. He didn't honor Jesus while he was alive, but perhaps he could honor him in his death. It was a brave move to risk being caught by the other Pharisees when there is no apparent gain now. It's a reminder that no matter what our past looks like, it's never too late to honor Jesus.

In John's gospel, we find out Joseph's pal Nicodemus tagged along. Nicodemus was also a secret follower of Jesus—the Pharisee who sought Jesus in the middle of the night (John 3:1-21). The duo had to prepare Jesus' body in haste. Once the sun went down, it would be the Sabbath, and they would no longer be permitted to work. So after wrapping the body in linen, they placed it in a tomb owned by Joseph, secured it with a stone, and then hurried home.

---

16 "Who Was Joseph of Arimathea?" GotQuestions.org, www.gotquestions.org/Joseph-of-Arimathea.html.

As far as they knew, the story of Jesus was over.

A Day of Darkness

The day after Jesus' death is known as Holy Saturday. It is a time of great despair for followers of Jesus. For us, it only lasts a day. We know the hope of Easter is around the corner. But to the people living the story out, this despair stretches on an endless road before them.

I like to imagine how the disciple Peter felt on Saturday. A day earlier, he denied knowing his friend and master (Station IV). He promised Jesus he would stick by him, and he failed. Then Peter gets word that Jesus has been crucified. This means he will never get the chance to redeem himself. The last interaction he had with Jesus will haunt him with shame for the rest of his life.

And what does he do now? Go back to being a fisherman and pretend the last three years of his life never happened? Does he try to forget Jesus and the things he's seen? Maybe someday it will all seem like a distant dream to Peter. That's the best he can hope for now—just a return to normalcy.

Saturday must have been a sleepless night for Peter. He thought things would only get worse. But then Easter morning came, and everything changed. Hope sprang forth from an empty tomb. And this hope made Friday and Saturday look completely different.

What's Your Saturday?

Are you living in despair that doesn't seem to have an end date?

I wrote this book while in the middle of the COVID-19 pandemic. There's a lot of uncertainty, and we don't know when life will return to normal. Is there hope? Yes. But we need to be careful not to use hope flippantly.

Sometimes people (especially Christians) throw out phrases like, "Everything will be okay," or "God is going to handle this all, so don't worry." We like to celebrate victories. We're not so good at sitting in Saturdays.

For many people in our communities and around the world, things will not be okay. Life is changed forever. People have lost their loved ones and aren't even able to mourn them with a proper memorial. They are figuring out how to move forward in life without a spouse, parent, child, or friend. For them, things will never go back to normal.

But I don't think the hope of Easter is to get back to a normal life. When Peter ran to the empty tomb on Sunday, he was forever changed. He couldn't go back to the person he was on Thursday before Jesus' arrest. The hope of Easter Sunday didn't erase the events of Friday and Saturday. But it did bring new meaning to them. It gave Peter a way to move forward. On Sunday, Jesus calls Peter and the rest of his followers to a bigger story. They've been invited to love like Jesus and live in a new way.

Life only got tougher for Peter after Easter. He would have to make many sacrifices, including giving up his own life in the end. *(Something most of the disciples were called to do.)* This new life would be hard, but it was worth it because of the hope of Easter. They had a Savior who blew the doors off death. They knew that because of Jesus, there was life waiting for them, even in suffering.

So even though we're only a page away from the hope of Easter, let's not be too quick to flip over to it. It's okay to sit in the pain of the cross a little while longer.

And in our personal Saturdays—the darkness we find ourselves in— let's remember the hope we have in Jesus. It's not a hope that promises everything will return to normal. It's a hope that Jesus has won the victory, so we can go out and love others.

And sometimes, that love looks like sitting in our Saturdays with other people.

💬 Questions to Ponder:

When have you hidden your devotion to Jesus like Joseph?

What "Saturday" are you in right now? What do you think is the difference between "flippant hope" and Easter hope?

What Saturdays are the people around you going through? How can you sit with them in it?

What is one thing you learned about Jesus from this station?

Station XV:
The Hope-Filled Tomb

Station XV of the Stations of the Cross: The Resurrection of Jesus.
Bible Reading: John 20:1-18

Mary ran and ran, all the way to the city… And it seemed to her that morning, as she ran, almost as if the whole world had been made anew, almost as if the whole world was singing for joy—the trees, tiny sounds in the grass, the birds… her heart. Was God really making everything sad come untrue? Was he even making death come untrue? She couldn't wait to tell Jesus' friends. "They won't believe it!" she laughed. She was right, of course. - From *The Jesus Storybook Bible* in the chapter "God's Wonderful Surprise."[17]

Not everyone loves surprises. But there are some surprises so wonderful they would make even the scroogiest among us crack a smile and jump for joy. Jesus' friends received one of these surprises on the first Easter Sunday.

We have finally reached the end of the *Via Dolorosa*. How are you feeling after the long, sorrowful journey? Reflecting on the sacrifice Jesus made for us is not always a pleasant experience. But, unbeknownst to Jesus' friends, the road of sorrows was always leading toward an empty tomb.

Well, the tomb wasn't entirely empty…

It was filled with hope!

---

17 *The Jesus Storybook Bible*, by Sally Lloyd-Jones, Zonderkidz, 2007, pp. 316–317.

An Unexpected Witness

All four gospel accounts approach the Easter story from different angles. John chose to focus his story on a poignant encounter between Mary Magdalene and Jesus. In a time when women were not allowed to be legal witnesses, Jesus chose Mary to be the first witness to his resurrection. Jesus was breaking down barriers and doing something new. I wonder how the world would change if we loved and included people the way Jesus did.

When Mary arrived at the tomb and saw that it was empty, she assumed someone stole Jesus' body. Every Easter Sunday, Pastor Andy Stanley quips, "Nobody expected no body." None of Jesus' friends woke up that morning expecting a miracle. Mary responds to the empty tomb the same way we would. She thought someone took Jesus' body because dead bodies aren't in the habit of moving themselves!

When Mary delivers this news to John and Peter, they rush to the tomb. John can't help throwing some shade at Peter when he writes, "They were both running, **but the other disciple outran Peter** and reached the tomb first" (v. 4, NLT, emphasis mine). I've said it before, but I'll say it again—humorous details like this are why I take the Bible seriously.

John and Peter have an interesting reaction when they get to the empty tomb:

*Then Simon Peter arrived and went inside. He also noticed the linen wrappings lying there, while the cloth that had covered Jesus' head was folded up and lying apart from the other wrappings. Then the disciple who had reached the tomb first also went in, and **he saw and believed—for until then they still hadn't understood the Scriptures that said Jesus must rise from the dead. Then they went home.*** (John 20:6-10, NLT, emphasis mine)

John and Peter see the empty tomb and "believe." But instead of jumping for joy, they go back home as if nothing has changed.

I think these two guys are caught between belief and doubt. It's such a human place to be. They believe, yet they also think this surprise is too wonderful to be true. So they go home.

It reminds me of the two disciples Jesus meets on the road to Emmaus. They have heard the news that Jesus is alive and are amazed by it. And yet, "sadness [was] written across their faces" (Luke 24:17, NLT).

Is it possible to believe and yet still have doubts? I think John, Peter, and all of Jesus' early followers would say yes.

Sitting in Sadness

Peter and John go home, but Mary stays by the tomb. She doesn't know what to do next. All she knows is she misses Jesus.

Mary had followed Jesus down much of the *Via Dolorosa*. She saw the agony of the cross firsthand. She watched her friend get tortured and humiliated, and there was nothing she could do to stop it. How many tears did she cry over the past 48 hours? Now, in the quiet stillness of the morning, Mary chooses to sit in her sadness.

And that's when she receives a wonderful surprise.

She turned to leave and saw someone standing there. It was Jesus, but she didn't recognize him. "Dear woman, why are you crying?" Jesus asked her. "Who are you looking for?"

She thought he was the gardener. "Sir," she said, "if you have taken him away, tell me where you have put him, and I will go and get him."

"Mary!" Jesus said.

She turned to him and cried out, "Rabboni!" (which is Hebrew for "Teacher").

"Don't cling to me," Jesus said, "for I haven't yet ascended to the Father. But go find my brothers and tell them, 'I am ascending to my Father and your Father, to my God and your God.'" (John 20:14-17, NLT)

There's something wonderfully fitting about Mary mistaking Jesus for a gardener. The journey down the Way of Sorrows began in a garden with Jesus sweating blood. Now we end the journey in another garden with Jesus conquering victory over death.

Mary didn't recognize Jesus at first. Maybe she couldn't see through her tear-filled eyes. Maybe her grief was keeping her from seeing hope. Or maybe Jesus just wanted to give her a really good surprise! No matter the reason, Jesus opens Mary's eyes with one word.

Mary.

Imagine the feeling of Jesus saying your name when you are at your lowest point. Imagine the hope that flooded Mary's heart. Commenting on this story, Charles Spurgeon said, "Jesus can preach a perfect sermon in one word."

When Jesus calls Mary by name, it changes everything. Mary feels known by Jesus. When we feel known by Jesus, it changes things for us too. This story is an encouragement that in times of grief and despair, Jesus calls out to us by name.

Christianity as we know it began with this intimate moment between Jesus and Mary. Outside the tomb, the world was rolling on as if nothing extraordinary happened. The Roman government thought one more criminal had been executed. The religious leaders thought they got rid of a troublemaker. Jesus' friends thought the story was over. They had no idea what Mary was experiencing in the early hours of this dreary morning.

Mary was a messy, broken human, just like you and me. But she was about to let the world in on life-changing news.

Mary Couldn't Keep Jesus to Herself

As I read some commentaries on these verses, I was surprised to learn how much debate there was about why Jesus didn't want Mary to "cling to [him]" (v. 17).

Some people think Jesus didn't want to be defiled in his newly resurrected state. But Jesus never avoids messes. He didn't suddenly become averse to hugs! I love the way Sally Lloyd-Jones puts Jesus' words in *The Jesus Storybook Bible*:

"You'll be able to hold on to me later, Mary," Jesus said gently, "and always be close to me. But now, go and tell the others that I'm alive!"[18]

I'm sure Jesus relished that quiet moment with Mary as much as Mary did. But Jesus knew he'd get to spend eternity with Mary. At that moment, he wanted her to share the life-changing hope she experienced.

And that's what Mary did. She ran back and told the disciples Jesus was alive. She ran back and told them because she knew Jesus didn't want anyone left out of his wonderful story.

The author of the book of Hebrews tells us Jesus traveled the Way of Sorrows "For the joy set before him" (Hebrews 12:2, NIV). And what was that joy?

You. Me. And all the other messy, broken people in this world.

The hope of Easter reminds us that Jesus came for messy, broken people.

Jesus traveled the Way of Sorrows because he didn't want you or me to travel the broken road alone. He traveled the Way of Sorrows because he loves us too much to allow Death to get the final word.

---

18 *The Jesus Storybook Bible*, by Sally Lloyd-Jones, Zonderkidz, 2007, p. 314.

As I reflect on the empty tomb, my prayer is to follow in the footsteps of Mary. I want to spend time with Jesus and be known by him. And then I want to share the wonderful surprise that he is alive with everyone I meet...

Because Jesus doesn't want anyone left out!

💬 Questions to Ponder:

Why do you think John and Peter went home after seeing the empty tomb? Have you ever been caught between belief and doubt?

How do you think Mary felt when Jesus called her by name? How does it make you feel to know Jesus knows you by name?

The hope-filled tomb is a reminder that Jesus loves you, no matter where you find yourself in life. How can you remind yourself of that on days when it doesn't feel true?

As your journey down the Way of Sorrows ends, do you see Jesus in any new ways? How did this journey bring you closer to him?

A Small Favor...

Thank you so much for reading *Nobody Left Out: Jesus & the Way of Sorrows*. Now that you've finished reading it, I would love to get your thoughts. It would mean a lot to me if you left an honest review on Amazon.

As you may know, Amazon reviews play an essential role in reaching other readers. They help people decide whether or not this book is right for them. Reviews also help me gain insight into the things I got right, and the areas I need to improve. I want to get better as a writer!

Based on your review, I'll continue tweaking this book's content and putting out new editions. It will also help me as I write future devotional books.

Feel free to leave a review at:

NobodyLeftOut.net/ReviewWayBook.

Thank you!

About the Author

Michael Murray is just a messy, broken guy trying to follow Jesus one step at a time. He was born with cerebral palsy, a disability that affects motor skills. Living life with CP has given Michael a unique perspective on God's grace and mercy. He created the *Nobody Left Out* book series to share the good news that every single person matters to Jesus.

Michael lives in Orlando, Florida, with his wife Diana (who's an amazing artist!) and their dog Ruby. He attends Summit Church, where he serves as a writer and actor on the family productions team. Michael is a big fan of sweet tea, musicals, and writing about himself in the third person.

Connect with Michael:

Website: NobodyLeftOut.net
Twitter: Twitter.com/MJ_Murray83
Facebook: Facebook.com/NobodyLeftOut
Instagram: Instagram.com/MichaelJMurray83

8 Encounters With Jesus

I sincerely hope this book helped you engage with Jesus in a fresh way. If you'd like to explore more stories about Jesus, you may enjoy reading *Nobody Left Out: Jesus Meets the Messes*. This 40-day devotional looks at eight encounters Jesus had with messy, broken people.

The eight stories we'll be walking through together are:

Encounter I: Jesus Meets The Lonely Thief
Encounter II: Jesus Meets The Know-It-All
Encounter III: Jesus Meets The Unwelcome Dinner Guest
Encounter IV: Jesus Meets The Woman Who Was Exploited
Encounter V: Jesus Meets The Sick Woman & The Dead Girl
Encounter VI: Jesus Meets The Blind Man With Perfect Vision
Encounter VII: Jesus Sees The Invisible Widow
Encounter VIII: Jesus Meets The Honest Criminal

You can order your copy of *Nobody Left Out: Jesus Meets the Messes* here:

NobodyLeftOut.net/Book

You can get the first five chapters of the book for free here:

NobodyLeftOut.net/Free

Special Thanks

I would like to thank the following people whose financial contributions made this book possible:

Robert Eichelberger

Mary Lee Carter

Del Schwalls

William Fielder

Beth Marshall

Marie Murray (Mom!)

Mike Ensley

Wilson Woodyard

Joshua Outing

Joe Savy (Uncle Joe!)

Vincent Patino

O.J. Aldrich

Dave Dickens

Nathanial Greenough

Mark and Yvonne Engwall

Randall Halley

Lindsey Cornett

Helinfield Hanecak

Richard McDonald

Margaret Kennedy-Ross

Mary Cooke

Leslie LaPlume

Tracey Perdue

Kristie Lynn

Joseph Mary Cao Nhan Do

Robert Braun

Karen L. Silvester

Rob Archangel

Gretchen Magner

Alicia Carey

Ingrid Bergmann

Sarah Chavez

Julie Christus

James A Bowen

Dawnique Savala

Anne Fabian

Rich & Nancy Wood

Ronnie Andrews Jr.

Lisa Johnson

Carlos Corredor

Lynda Duncan

Amanda Richards

Miriam Wilson

Lindsay Cosmen